SAUCES

BLOOMSBURY

This edition first published 1988
Bloomsbury Publishing Limited
2 Soho Square
London W1V 5DE

English edition translated and produced by Malcolm Saunders Publishing Ltd
and Rosemary Wilkinson
26 Ornan Road
London NW3 4QB

Reprinted 1991

British Library Cataloguing in Publication Data
Sauces.
1. Sauces – Recipes
641.8'14

ISBN 0–7475–0281–1

Typeset by Fakenham Photosetting Ltd
Printed in Hong Kong

FOREWORD

A cook who produces successful sauces is often regarded as some sort of a magician in the kitchen. But sauce-making does not rely on supernatural powers: it's a matter of mastering certain basic skills and having the courage to give free rein to the imagination when it comes to the flavourings. Creativity and a good sauce are inseparable.

There are two essential considerations when making a sauce. Firstly, the basic raw ingredients of the sauce must shine through in the end product and secondly, the finished sauce should emphasize and enhance the taste of the food it accompanies, never disguise or mask it.

A tasty sauce can make an interesting meal of simple and inexpensive food. Grilled fish or potatoes, for example, can be magnificent with a good sauce.

If you are unsure about making sauces, choose the simple recipes to begin with. These have been given the one cook's head symbol.

This symbol is a guide for those interested in making the more advanced sauces. They need a little extra time and care, but the results will be magnificent.

Skilled sauce-makers have the complete range of over 200 wonderful sauces at their fingertips.

NOTE
1. 1 tsp = 1 teaspoon = 5 ml
   1 tbs = 1 tablespoon = 15 ml

2. The metric and imperial measurements are not exact equivalents, so follow one or other within a recipe but do not mix them.

CONTENTS

An ordinary aluminium saucepan or stainless steel saucepan is perfect for making sauce in. But if you use an aluminium saucepan, do not mix with a metal whisk as this may discolour the sauce. Use a wooden spoon or a wooden fork.

A stainless steel sieve with a well-rounded bottom is ideal for sieving sauces when all the ingredients are to be pressed through to form a purée. Use a spoon to press through the last few bits.

A wooden spoon and a wooden fork or spatula are useful for sauces that need to be well stirred. The straight sides of the spatula or fork facilitate the scraping of the sides and the bottom of a saucepan.

A conical sieve is perfect for separating solids and liquids, e.g. if peppercorns or other large spices are to be sieved off.

A shallow, straight-sided saucepan is useful for cooking certain types of sauces. It will maintain a steady even heat. Stainless steel ensures that a sauce will not discolour.

The high speed of this metal whisk gives the sauce a wonderful lightness, even without much butter. Whisk the sauce whilst still in the saucepan just before serving.

Before you know the measures off by heart, measuring spoons are indispensable. Keep them at hand in the kitchen.

A multi-stranded, flexible balloon whisk gives excellent results on light sauces. Choose a well-balanced whisk in stainless steel and test how good it feels in your hand.

A spiral whisk will get into the corners of a flat-bottomed saucepan. The whole sauce is kept in movement and nothing is burnt.

A one-portion ladle is an ideal piece of equipment to have to hand.

A food-processor is a time and labour-saving piece of equipment for all stages of sauce making, from the initial chopping of the ingredients to the final puréeing.

THE CONTRIBUTION OF THE DAIRY TO SAUCE MAKING

Certain ingredients play key roles in making a sauce. Herbs and spices bring a distinctive flavour to a sauce (and these are discussed on page 70); dairy products have a more subtle function, either accentuating the aromatic properties of the other flavourings or smoothing and enriching the final overall taste.

BUTTER is a particularly good taste carrier. Take curry powder, for example. In its tin or packet it has a raw, dry smell but sizzle it in butter and the most fantastic aromas are released. It is helpful to use unsalted butter, as this allows you greater control over the amount of salt in the final result.

CREAM works miracles in sauces through its quality of combining and enriching all the tastes and aromas of the raw materials.

CRÈME FRAÎCHE is excellent in both warm and cold sauces, particularly in fish sauces. It makes the sauce creamy and gives a slightly acid taste which is delicious. A low-calorie version is especially good for slimmers.

The fresh, sharp taste of SOUR CREAM is the perfect basis for cold, modern, light sauces. It has the consistency of double cream without the higher calories. With appropriate flavourings it makes marvellous sauces for salads, fish, seafood and meat.

QUARK is a smooth, fresh cheese. It is a cousin to cottage cheese but has even less fat. A cold sauce made with quark will be low in fat without being thin in texture. It can be diluted to pouring consistency with milk, buttermilk or single cream.

MILK has its obvious place in sauce-making. A creamy, thickened milk sauce provides the basis for a huge variety of added flavourings. Semi-skimmed and skimmed milks will help keep the calories down.

The slight acidity and fresh taste of YOGURT give an exciting flavour to salad dressings, with the bonus that the sauce will be low in calories.

BASIC SAUCES AND THICKENINGS

MASTER THE ART OF PRODUCING A SMALL NUMBER OF BASIC SAUCES AND THE HORIZONS ARE EXTENDED FOR ALL SORTS OF DELICIOUS SAUCES.

THE BASIC SAUCE IS THE STARTING POINT FOR YOUR OWN CREATIVITY.

ON THE NEXT FEW PAGES THE MOST COMMON SAUCES ARE DESCRIBED STEP BY STEP.

TO OBTAIN THE DESIRED CONSISTENCY, MANY SAUCES NEED TO BE THICKENED. THICKENINGS ARE GIVEN ON PAGES 12 AND 13.

BASIC WHITE SAUCE – BÉCHAMEL SAUCE

This sauce is based on milk. All types of milk can be used. The sauce is prepared with plain flour and, in this case, with a roux (see page 13) but the sauce can also be prepared using a flour paste thickening (see page 13). A white sauce is the foundation of many delicious sauces. To make about four servings of basic white sauce:

2 tbs butter
2 tbs flour
400 ml (14 fl oz) milk

Melt the butter slowly in a saucepan. Add the flour.

Stir the butter and the flour and allow them to sizzle together a little.

Pour in the milk, little by little, stirring all the time.

Cook the sauce for at least 3–5 minutes, so that it doesn't taste of flour. Add flavourings, if desired.

Try the following quick and easy flavourings:

2–3 tbs of finely-chopped fresh parsley or
2–3 tbs of grated horseradish or
1 tbs of made mustard or
1–2 tbs smoked cod's roe paste

Finally, add a little salt and pepper to the sauce.

BASIC WHITE SAUCE WITHOUT FAT

This is a low calorie version. Naturally, since the butter is omitted, the flavour will be bland compared to the normal white sauce but this can be compensated for by adding interesting flavourings. To make approximately four servings use:

400 ml (14 fl oz) milk
2 tbs flour

Mix the milk and the flour in a saucepan.

Bring the sauce to the boil, whisking all the time. Cook the sauce for 3–5 minutes, then add salt and pepper to taste.

Here are a few suggestions for flavourings:

55 g (2 oz) blue cheese or
2–3 tbs grated horseradish or
1 tbs tomato purée or
1–2 tbs smoked cod's roe paste

Add salt and pepper to taste.

LIGHT BASIC SAUCE – VELOUTÉ SAUCE

This sauce is made with a light stock from, for example, goose, chicken, fish or vegetables. The sauce is thickened with plain flour. An egg yolk or a little cream can also be added to give a fuller and richer taste. To make about four servings of light basic sauce:

2 tbs butter
2 tbs flour
400 ml (14 fl oz) light stock

Melt the butter slowly in a saucepan.

Add the flour.

Stir and let the butter and the flour sizzle together a little.

Pour in the stock, little by little, stirring all the time.

Cook the sauce for 3–5 minutes, so that it doesn't taste of flour.

A sauce velouté is an ideal starting point for many good sauces. Here are a few suggestions for flavourings:

1–2 tbs squeezed lemons or
1–2 tbs tomato purée or
½–1 tsp curry powder (sizzle that together with the butter, see first picture) or
½ fresh red or green pepper chopped in cubes

Taste the sauce and add salt and pepper if necessary.

BASIC BROWN SAUCE – SAUCE ESPAGNOLE

For this sauce, use a brown stock made from, for example, red meat. As with the light basic sauce, this sauce is also thickened with plain flour. It is seldom served on its own but is the vehicle for a wide variety of flavourings. To make a basic brown sauce for about four servings:

2 tbs butter
2 tbs flour
400 ml (14 fl oz) brown stock

Melt the butter slowly in a saucepan.

Add the flour.

Mix the flour and the butter and let them sizzle together a little.

Pour in the stock, little by little, stirring continuously.

Cook the sauce for 3–5 minutes, so that it doesn't taste of flour.

Experiment with different flavourings, starting with the following:

1–2 tbs tomato purée or
½ fresh red or green pepper in cubes or
1–2 tbs port or madeira

Taste the sauce, add salt and pepper if necessary.

GRAVY

Gravy is made from the meat juices released during roasting, casseroling, braising or frying. It is important that there are no burnt pieces in the juices as these will spoil the flavour. Remove any fat before you begin making the sauce. This is easiest to do if you let the meat juices stand a while so that the fat rises to the top. If the amount of meat juice is insufficient, dilute with a little stock. To make gravy for about four servings:

200 ml (7 fl oz) meat juices or stock
2 tbs plain flour
1½ tbs cold water
gravy browning, if desired

Boil up the meat juices and the stock (if used).

Whisk the water and the flour together in a bowl. Pour the thickening in a fine stream into the saucepan, whisking continuously.

Cook the sauce for 3–5 minutes. Add a little gravy browning mixed with water if a darker colour is required.

Various flavourings can now be added, for example:

1–2 tbs freshly-squeezed lemon juice or
1–2 tbs orange juice or
1 tbs madeira or port or
1–2 tbs tomato purée or
1 tsp crushed pink peppercorns and
salt and pepper

BEURRE BLANC – BUTTER SAUCE

Beurre Blanc is a classic butter sauce. Other fine butter sauces are, for example, Béarnaise (page 45) and Hollandaise (page 63). Béarnaise sauce has a slightly acid taste and a full flavour from the tarragon used. It is also flavoured with parsley. Hollandaise sauce is a little milder in taste and less acid. To make 4–6 portions of Beurre Blanc:

3 shallots
3 tbs white wine vinegar
100 ml (3½ fl oz) white wine or water
255 g (9 oz) butter at room temperature
salt, white pepper and freshly-squeezed lemon juice

Chop the shallots very finely. Mix them with the vinegar and the wine or water in a saucepan. Boil and reduce the liquid by half.

Strain to remove the onion. Lower the heat. Add the butter in small amounts. Whisk vigorously until all the butter is blended in.

Flavour the sauce with salt, pepper and lemon juice.

MAYONNAISE

Mayonnaise is not difficult to make as long as the oil is added carefully and whisked in thoroughly. It is a good idea to have all the ingredients at the same temperature. To make mayonnaise:

2 egg yolks
½ tsp salt
¼ tsp white pepper
2 tsp vinegar
285 ml (10 fl oz) oil
freshly-squeezed lemon juice

Put the egg yolks into a bowl. Add salt, pepper and vinegar. Whisk them together fast and thoroughly.

Add the oil, at first drop by drop, then in a fine stream, whisking continuously.

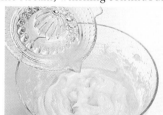

Add the lemon juice for flavouring.

The easiest way to make mayonnaise is with a food processor. Put the egg yolks, salt, pepper and vinegar into the food processor and turn on. Pour in the oil, little by little, as the machine is still running. For a lighter and airier mayonnaise, mix in some whipped or sour cream.

VINAIGRETTE

This dressing is a classic which tastes as good natural as it does flavoured. The normal proportion of vinegar to oil is one to three but do make your own mixture as you prefer it. Use the dressing only when it is fresh. To make vinaigrette:

1 tbs vinegar
¼ tsp salt
¼ tsp pepper
3 tbs olive oil or 2 tbs oil + 1 tbs water

Pour the vinegar into a bowl or directly into a salad dressing bottle. Add salt, pepper and any chosen flavourings.

Add the oil or the oil and water. Stir or shake together.

Here are a few suggestions for flavourings:

1 tsp mustard or
½–1 squeezed clove garlic or
2 tbs finely-chopped mixture of fresh parsley, dill, tarragon and chervil or
1 tsp salad seasoning or seasoning salt

FLOUR THICKENING

This thickening is ideal for sauces made from fats left in the pan after frying onion or meat. The flour absorbs the fats before liquid is added. To make a flour thickening suitable for 300–400 g (11–14 oz) meat:

2 tbs plain flour
285–340 ml (10–12 fl oz) milk or cream

Fry the meat. Stir in the flour.

Add milk or cream, little by little, stirring continuously. Stir for at least 3–5 minutes.

BEURRE MANIÉ

Beurre manié is used to thicken sauces and casseroles. It is ideal to add to sauces which are too thin. Add the beurre manié bit by bit until the desired consistency is reached. To make a beurre manié thickening suitable for 400 ml (14 fl oz) sauce:

2 tbs softened butter
2 tbs flour

Mix together the butter and the flour.

Add the mixture bit by bit to the sauce over a medium heat, whisking all the time. Let the sauce cook for another 3–5 minutes.

FLOUR PASTE THICKENING

By this method the thickening agents are added to the completed sauce. It is therefore suitable for a sauce which is too thin. To make a flour paste thickening for about 400 ml (14 fl oz) of sauce:

3 tbs water
2 tbs flour

Whisk together the water and the flour in a bowl.

Pour the flour mixture into the sauce over a medium heat, whisking continuously. Cook the sauce for another 3–5 minutes.

BASIC ROUX

This method is used at the start of a sauce recipe. The sauce is thickened by adding the liquid ingredients to a roux, i.e., a mixture of flour and fat. To make a roux suitable for 400 ml (14 fl oz) of sauce:

2 tbs butter
2 tbs flour

Melt the butter slowly in a saucepan. Add the flour and stir.

Let them sizzle together a little.

Pour in the sauce little by little, stirring all the time. Cook the sauce for another 3–5 minutes.

DRESSINGS FOR SALADS

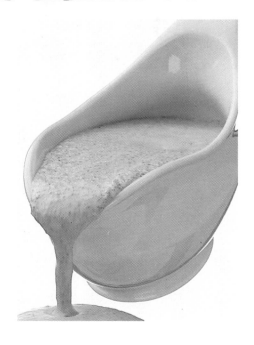

PINK PEPPER DRESSING

200 ml (7 fl oz) crème fraîche or sour cream,
1–2 tsp dried pink peppercorns, salt.

Spoon the crème fraîche or the sour cream
directly into a serving dish.

Crush the pink peppercorns in a mortar.

Mix in the pepper, add salt to taste. Chill
the dressing for one hour before serving.
This is suitable for all salads, also for fried
meat, fish or chicken.

Serves 4

SOUR CREAM WITH TOMATO

200 ml (7 fl oz) sour cream, 2–3 tsp chilli
sauce, 1 tsp tomato ketchup, 1 peeled clove
garlic, lemon pepper, Tabasco sauce.

Pour the sour cream into a bowl and mix in
the chilli sauce and tomato ketchup.

Squeeze the garlic and mix well.

Add the lemon pepper and Tabasco to taste.
Chill before serving.
Delicious with lettuce, cucumber and
potato salad.

Serves 4

HOT CHILLI DRESSING

100 ml (3½ fl oz) quark, 1 peeled clove
garlic, 55 ml (2 fl oz) spicy tomato ketchup
and, if desired, 55 ml (2 fl oz) milk.

Spoon the quark into a bowl. Squeeze the
garlic into it.

Mix in the spicy tomato ketchup.

For a thinner dressing, dilute with the milk.
Chill before serving.
This dressing is delicious with salad,
cauliflower, crudités, cooked white beans
and with white cabbage.

Serves 3–4

GOURMET SALAD DRESSING

200 ml (7 fl oz) whipping cream
100 ml (3½ fl oz) mayonnaise
1–2 tbs freshly-squeezed lemon juice
½ tsp salt
1 tsp sugar
1 freshly-squeezed clove garlic
few drops Tabasco sauce
pinch cayenne pepper
2–3 tsp chilli sauce
1 tbs sherry

Whip the cream and mix it with the other
ingredients. Chill the sauce for several
hours before serving.
This sauce is ideal for all salads.

Serves 6

CRANKS' DRESSING

1 tbs vinegar
1½ tbs water
1½ tbs oil
100 ml (3½ fl oz) natural yogurt or sour
cream
¼ tsp salt
pinch white pepper
2 tsp mustard

Mix together the vinegar, water, oil and
yogurt or sour cream. Season with salt,
pepper and mustard. Mix with alfalfa
sprouts if desired.
This is delicious for all salads and crudités.

Serves 4

MUSTARD DRESSING

2 hard-boiled eggs
1 tbs mustard, preferably sugar-free
1 tbs freshly-squeezed lemon juice
½ tsp salt
pinch black pepper
3 tbs whipped cream
1 tbs chopped chives

Separate the egg yolks from the whites.
Whip the egg yolks together with the
mustard. Add the lemon juice. Add salt and
pepper to taste, then add the cream and the
chopped chives. Chop up the egg whites
and sprinkle them on top of the dressing.
Pour the dressing over your favourite salad.

Serves 2–3

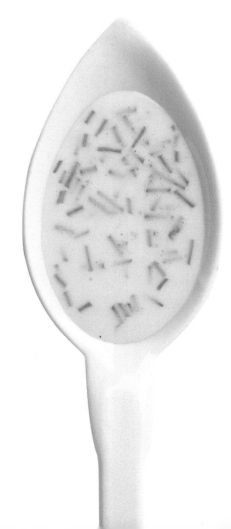

CUCUMBER DRESSING

1 cucumber (about 20 cm/8 in long)
285 ml (10 fl oz) crème fraîche
salt and white pepper
approx. 2 tbs finely-chopped fresh tarragon
or chervil

Slice the cucumber into pieces and run them
through a food processor or liquidizer. Add
the crème fraîche. Add the seasoning and
herbs to taste, then sieve the dressing
through a fine sieve.
Ideal for all salads.

Serves 6

DILL AND TOMATO DRESSING

100 ml (3½ fl oz) tomato juice
200 ml (7 fl oz) whipping cream
2–3 tbs dill seeds or 3–4 fresh dill seed
heads
salt and pepper

Boil the tomato juice. Add the cream and
the dill. Let the sauce cook for 4–5 minutes,
then add salt and pepper to taste. Sieve the
dressing and let it cool.
Ideal for most salads.

Serves 6

WALNUT DRESSING

200 ml (7 fl oz) sour cream
3 tbs chopped walnuts
3 tbs finely-chopped fresh parsley
1 tsp white wine vinegar
¼ tsp black pepper
salt

Mix the sour cream with the walnuts,
parsley, vinegar and pepper. Add salt to
taste.
This dressing brings out the taste of lettuce,
avocado, cucumber and cauliflower.

Serves 4

DIJON DRESSING

1 shallot, 200 ml (7 fl oz) sour cream, 1 tbs mild mustard.

Chop the shallot very finely.

Pour the sour cream into a bowl and add the shallot.

Add the mustard and stir well. Chill before serving.
Ideal for green salads and tomatoes.

Serves 4

DILL DRESSING

200 ml (7 fl oz) sour cream, 1 tsp crushed cumin, 1 tsp mild mustard, 6 tbs finely-chopped fresh dill.

Pour the sour cream into a bowl.

Spice with the cumin and the mustard.

Chop the dill finely and mix it in. Chill the dressing before serving.
Pour this dressing over green salads and tomatoes.

Serves 4

MAYONNAISE DRESSING

100 ml (3½ fl oz) mayonnaise, 100 ml (3½ fl oz) milk, 55 ml (2 fl oz) spicy tomato ketchup, 1 tsp dried tarragon.

Pour the mayonnaise and the milk into a bowl.

Whisk the mixture until it becomes smooth.

Mix in the spicy tomato ketchup.

Crush the tarragon and mix in well.
This dressing is good for all sorts of salads.

Serves 4–6

TOMATO MUSTARD CREAM

200 ml (7 fl oz) sour cream, 100 ml (3½ fl oz) milk, 2 tbs mustard, 2 tbs tomato ketchup, ½ tsp ground allspice, 3 tbs dill.

Mix the sour cream and milk in a bowl.

Add the mustard, ketchup and the allspice.

Chop the dill finely and mix in.

Whisk the dressing until it is smooth, then serve with any kind of workaday salad, such as grated carrots, white cabbage salad, rice salad, macaroni salad.

Serves 4–6

APPLE DRESSING

1 large apple, 200 ml (7 fl oz) sour cream, 1–2 tbs grated horseradish, 1 tsp vinegar, ½ tsp sugar.

The apple can be grated with or without its skin. Do not grate in any of the core.

Mix quickly with the sour cream and the horseradish.

Add vinegar and sugar to taste.
This is delicious with lettuce and potato salads.

Serves 4

GARLIC DRESSING

200 ml (7 fl oz) sour cream, 3 tbs parsley, 1–2 peeled cloves garlic, salt and pepper.

Pour the sour cream directly into the serving bowl.

Chop the parsley finely and mix into the sour cream.

Crush the garlic into the dish and add salt and pepper to taste. Chill the dressing for about 30 minutes before serving.
This dressing is good with green salads, crudités, boiled white beans and fresh mushrooms.

Serves 4

19

GARDENER'S DRESSING

100 ml (3½ fl oz) crème fraîche, 55 g (2 oz) frozen spinach, thawed and drained, 1 peeled clove garlic, 2 tbs fresh parsley, 2 tbs fresh dill, 1–2 tbs capers, 100 ml (3½ fl oz) sour cream, sprig tarragon, salt, pepper.

Put the cream, spinach, garlic, parsley, dill and capers into the food processor.

Add the sour cream.

Add the tarragon and process until the sauce is smooth. Add salt and pepper to taste.
This is good for all sorts of salads.

Serves 4

AMERICAN SALAD DRESSING

3 tbs spicy tomato ketchup, 55 ml (2 fl oz) crème fraîche, 140 ml (5 fl oz) sour cream, 8 drops Worcestershire sauce.

Pour the spicy tomato ketchup and the crème fraîche into a food processor.

Add the sour cream.

Drop the Worcestershire sauce in and process until the sauce is smooth. This sauce adds a bite to all salads.

Serves 4

CAESAR DRESSING

2 tsp capers, 6 rolled sardine fillets, 1 peeled clove garlic, 100 ml (3½ fl oz) sour cream, 100 ml (3½ fl oz) crème fraîche, 1 egg yolk, 1 tsp mustard powder.

Put the capers, sardines, garlic, sour cream and crème fraîche into the food processor.

Add the egg yolk.

Spice with the mustard powder and process until the sauce is smooth.
Pour the sauce over lettuce mixed with fried bread cubes.

Serves 4

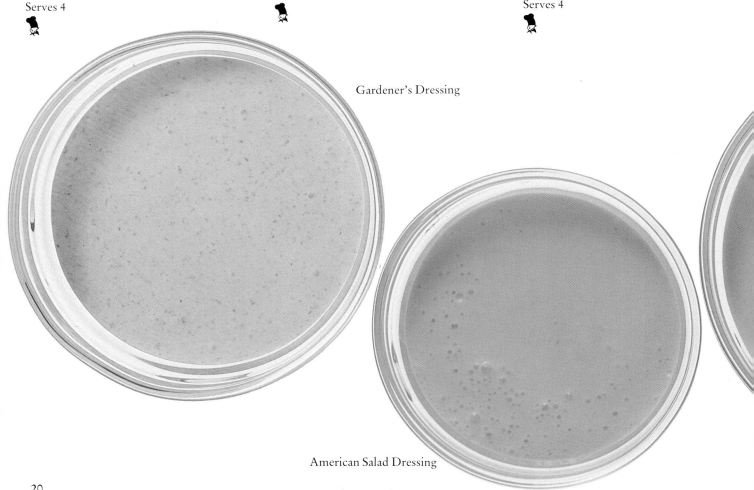

Gardener's Dressing

American Salad Dressing

20

RUSSIAN SALAD DRESSING

1 medium-sized pickled beetroot, 1 tbs baby pickled onions, 200 ml (7 fl oz) sour cream, 1 tbs capers.

Put the beetroot and the pickled onion into the food processor.

Add the sour cream.

Add the capers. Run the machine for just a few seconds so that the sauce remains slightly lumpy.
Particularly good with green salads and crudités.

Serves 4

HOT MADRAS DRESSING

1 tsp chilli sauce, 1 tbs curry powder, 1 tbs chutney, 200 ml (7 fl oz) sour cream, a few drops of Tabasco sauce.

Put the chilli sauce, curry and chutney into a food processor.

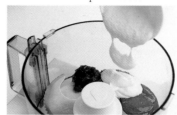

Add the sour cream.

Drop in the Tabasco and process until the dressing is smooth.
This dressing adds a bite to all kinds of green salads.

Serves 4

SOUR CREAM AND BLUE CHEESE

55 g (2 oz) blue cheese, 3 tbs chopped walnuts, 55 ml (2 fl oz) sour cream, salt.

Break up the blue cheese into pieces and put in the food processor. Add the walnuts.

Add the sour cream and process until the whole mixture is well blended.

Add salt to taste.
This sauce is good with lettuce, cucumber and fresh mushrooms.

Serves 4

Russian Salad Dressing

Hot Madras Dressing

Caesar Dressing

AVOCADO CREAM

1 ripe avocado
200 ml (7 fl oz) sour cream or crème fraîche
1 tsp freshly-squeezed lemon juice

Cut the avocado in half, peel and remove the stone. Mash it up using a fork and mix with the sour cream or crème fraîche and lemon juice. This can also be done in a food processor or a liquidizer.
This is very nice with green salads and fresh mushroms.

Serves 4

CELERIAC DRESSING

200 ml (7 fl oz) sour cream
2 tbs mayonnaise
6 tbs grated celeriac
½ tsp salt
¼–½ tsp black pepper, coarsely ground if possible
1–2 tsp mustard

Mix the sour cream and the mayonnaise. Grate the celeriac and immediately mix with the sour cream to prevent browning. Season with salt, pepper and mustard.
Delicious with all salads, particularly with hard-boiled egg. Also good with meat pâté.

Serves 4

ROSÉ HERB DRESSING

200 ml (7 fl oz) sour cream
3 tbs rosé wine
1–2 tbs dried tarragon
1–2 tbs dried chervil
or double the amount of chopped, fresh herbs
salt

Mix all the ingredients together. Leave the sauce to chill for a few hours in the fridge before serving. Add salt to taste.
Good with all salads.

Serves 4

PINK SALAD DRESSING

6–7 tbs sunflower seeds
water
1 small fresh beetroot
200 ml (7 fl oz) quark
1 peeled garlic clove
1 tsp seasoning salt

Liquidize the sunflower seeds with a little water in a food processor or liquidizer. Add the beetroot, chopped into pieces, and the quark. Squeeze the garlic and add to the mixture. Run the food processor until the sauce becomes creamy. Add seasoning salt to taste.
Good with all salads.

Serves 4

QUICK DIP

200–285 ml (7–10 fl oz) sour cream
1–2 tsp Italian salad seasoning
½ tsp salt
¼ tsp black pepper
1 tsp curry powder or paprika
¼ tsp sugar, if desired

Mix the sour cream with all the other ingredients and stir well. Chill the sauce for at least 30 minutes before serving.
Use this dip for carrots, cucumber, fresh mushrooms and toast or crispbread.

Serves 4–6

OLD-FASHIONED SALAD DRESSING

140 ml (5 fl oz) whipping cream
1–2 tbs freshly-squeezed lemon juice or vinegar
½ tbs sugar
1 tsp mustard
salt and white pepper

Mix together the cream, the lemon juice or vinegar, the sugar and the mustard, then season with salt and pepper, to taste.
This adds a fine flavouring to green salads and crudités.

Serves 4

BLUE CHEESE VINAIGRETTE

40 g (1½ oz) blue cheese
1 tbs sherry vinegar
5 tbs quark
1 tbs finely-chopped chives
2 tbs walnut oil
salt and freshly ground pepper

Mash the cheese with a fork and mix it in a bowl with the other ingredients. Add salt and pepper carefully, as the cheese is rather salty.
Lovely on a plain salad with roast walnuts.

Serves 4

TOMATO AND CHILLI DRESSING

6 medium-sized ripe tomatoes
100 ml (3½ fl oz) crème fraîche
2 tsp red chilli pepper, very finely sliced
fresh, finely-chopped basil
salt and freshly ground pepper

Purée the tomatoes in a food processor or a liquidizer. Sieve to remove the seeds and skin. Stir in the crème fraîche with the chilli pepper and the basil. Add salt and pepper to taste.
Delicious on tomato salad garnished with chives.

Serves 4

CHILLI YOGURT DRESSING

200 ml (7 fl oz) natural yogurt
1 crushed clove garlic
a piece of cucumber, 5 cm (2 in) long, finely sliced
½–1 tsp red chilli pepper, very finely sliced
3 tbs chopped chives and fresh parsley
3 tbs walnuts
salt

Mix the yogurt, garlic, cucumber, chilli, parsley and chives together in a bowl. Dampen the walnuts with water and sprinkle with salt. Roast in the oven at 120° C/250° F/Gas Mark ½ for 10 minutes, then break the walnuts into pieces and stir into the dressing.
This dressing is beautiful with all green salads.

Serves 4

COS LETTUCE

Cos lettuce is a close cousin of the round lettuce. Its outer leaves are long and coarse. Before picking, the leaves are bound up, so that the inner leaves stay white and soft. It's available all year round but home-grown varieties come onto the market in summer. With its slightly stronger taste and crisp texture it is ideal in salads. The shape of the leaves also makes a perfect container for creamy sauces.

SAUCES FOR VEGETABLES

LEMON CREAM SAUCE

200 ml (7 fl oz) whipping cream, 1 tbs flour, ½ well-washed lemon, black pepper.

Mix the cream and the flour in a saucepan.

Cook for 3 minutes, stirring constantly.

Grate the lemon peel.

Mix the lemon peel into the sauce and add the black pepper.
Serve with boiled or steamed vegetables, particularly with asparagus, leeks and broccoli.

Serves 2–3

HOT CHEESE SAUCE

425 ml (15 fl oz) milk, 2 tbs flour, 170–225 g (6–8 oz) grated hard cheese, pepper.

Mix the flour and the milk in a saucepan.
Cook for 3 minutes, whisking constantly.

Grate the cheese.

Mix the cheese into the sauce and stir until it is melted. Do not let the sauce boil. Add the pepper, to taste.
This is particularly good with boiled vegetables, such as leeks and broccoli. Also good as a gratin sauce.

Serves 4

COD'S ROE SAUCE

425 ml (15 fl oz) milk, 2 tbs flour, 3 tbs chopped fresh dill, 2 tbs smoked cod's roe paste, 1–2 tbs butter, pepper.

Whisk the milk and flour in a saucepan.
Cook for 3 minutes, whisking constantly.

Add the dill and the cod's roe paste.

Add the butter, bit by bit, whisking all the time. Add pepper to taste.
Serve with boiled or steamed vegetables, such as cauliflower, swede and white cabbage.

Serves 4

WALNUT CREAM

200 ml (7 fl oz) crème fraîche, 1 tsp walnut oil if desired, 100 g (3½ oz) walnuts.

Spoon the crème fraîche into a bowl and add the oil if using.

Chop the walnuts finely.

Mix them with the crème fraîche and serve with boiled vegetables and vegetable pies.

Serves 3–4

COLD CHEESE SAUCE

30 g (1 oz) blue cheese, 100 ml (3½ fl oz) sour cream, 100 ml (3½ fl oz) crème fraîche, 2 tbs grated cheese (hard cheese or Parmesan), pinch grated nutmeg, pinch cayenne pepper.

Grate the blue cheese.

Mix the cheese with the sour cream and the crème fraîche.

Add the grated hard cheese with the nutmeg and cayenne pepper to taste. Mix well. Ideal for all boiled vegetables.

Serves 3–4

SCANDINAVIAN SKAGEN SAUCE

200 ml (7 fl oz) sour cream or quark
2 tbs mayonnaise
1 tbs spicy tomato ketchup
approx. 200 g (7 oz) finely-chopped prawns
3 tbs finely-chopped fresh dill
pepper
a little red lumpfish roe, if desired
lemon wedges

Mix the sour cream or quark with the mayonnaise and the spicy tomato ketchup. Add the prawns and the dill. Stir in pepper to taste. Serve with baked potatoes. A teaspoonful of lumpfish roe placed in each potato is delicious. Garnish with dill. Serve with the lemon wedges.

Serves 3–4

HAZELNUT HOLLANDAISE

200 g (7 oz) butter at room temperature
3 egg yolks
2 tbs water
¼ tsp cayenne pepper
1 tbs freshly-squeezed lemon juice
6 tbs chopped hazelnuts

Melt the butter carefully over a low heat, then set aside. Put a stainless steel bowl or saucepan into a larger saucepan containing hot but not boiling water. Put the egg yolks and the water into the bowl and whisk continuously, until the egg yolks become creamy. Take the saucepan off the heat. Whisk in the butter little by little. Add cayenne pepper and lemon juice to taste. Chop the hazelnuts coarsely and dry roast them in a non-stick pan, until evenly browned.
Pour the sauce over boiled vegetables and sprinkle the nuts on top. Serve immediately.

Serves 6

PIQUANT HERB SAUCE

2 shallots
55 ml (2 fl oz) white wine vinegar
55 ml (2 fl oz) white wine
110 ml (4 fl oz) whipping cream
155 g (5½ oz) unsalted butter at room temperature
30 g (1 oz) in total of the following herbs: parsley, dill, chervil and tarragon
salt and pepper

Chop the shallots finely and soften them in a little butter over a low heat. Add the vinegar and the white wine, and boil rapidly until reduced to one-third. Add the cream and cook for one minute. Mix in the butter little by little, then transfer to a food processor or liquidizer together with the herbs. Process until smooth. Add salt and pepper to taste.
This adds a fine flavour to boiled vegetables of all types.

Serves 4–6

CREAMY AVOCADO DRESSING

1 ripe avocado
1 crushed clove garlic
55 ml (2 fl oz) water
2 tsp oil, if desired
2 tbs crème fraîche
1 tbs finely-chopped fresh dill
½ tsp honey
½ tsp salt
2 tbs freshly-squeezed lemon juice

Purée the avocado in a food processor or a liquidizer, or pass it through a sieve. Add the other ingredients. Purée the whole mixture in the food processor or stir until the mixture becomes creamy and smooth. Excellent sauce for avocado and green salads.

Serves 2

COLD SAFFRON SAUCE

2 tbs butter, pinch of powdered saffron, 285 ml (15 fl oz) whipping cream, 100–140 ml (3½–5 fl oz) crème fraîche, salt and pepper, 1 tbs sesame seeds.

Melt the butter in a saucepan and add the saffron.

Simmer for a few minutes, then add the cream. Let the sauce simmer a few minutes more.

Stir in the crème fraîche.

Add salt and pepper to taste and sprinkle with the sesame seeds, which you have, in the meantime, dry-roasted.
Serve the sauce cold with boiled or steamed vegetables.

Serves 6

2-2-2 SAUCE

200 ml (7 fl oz) single cream or milk, 2 egg yolks, 200 g (7 oz) grated hard cheese, salt and pepper.

Pour the cream or milk into a saucepan and bring to the boil.

Take the saucepan off the heat. Add the egg yolks and the cheese. Whisk until the cheese has melted. Do not cook any further.

Add salt and pepper to taste.
Serve with boiled vegetables; especially good with leeks, broccoli and cauliflower.

Serves 4

PARTY BUTTER

55 g (2 oz) butter at room temperature, 3–4 tbs crème fraîche, 1–2 tsp freshly-squeezed lemon juice, a few drops of Tabasco sauce and salt if needed.

Put the butter into a bowl and soften with a fork.

Add the crème fraîche little by little, stirring constantly.

Add the lemon juice, Tabasco and possibly salt to taste.
Let the butter melt over freshly-boiled vegetables.

Serves 4

FROTHY SAUCE

2 tbs butter, 2 tbs flour, 200 ml (7 fl oz) vegetable stock, 200 ml (7 fl oz) milk, 2 egg yolks, salt and pepper, 1 tbs lemon juice, if desired, 100 ml (3½ fl oz) whipped cream.

Melt the butter in a saucepan. Mix in the flour and cook for 1 minute. Gradually stir in the stock and the milk.

Let the mixture cook gently for 3–5 minutes, stirring occasionally.

Take the saucepan off the heat and stir in the egg yolks. Add salt, pepper and perhaps the lemon juice to taste.

Finally, add the whipped cream and whisk the mixture until the sauce becomes frothy. Do not cook the sauce any longer. Pour over boiled vegetables.

Serves 4

HERB BUTTER

100 g (3½ oz) butter at room temperature
1–2 tsp freshly-squeezed lemon juice
1 finely-chopped clove garlic
2 tbs chopped fresh parsley
1 tsp salt
pinch white pepper

Mix the butter until it becomes soft. Stir in the lemon juice, garlic, parsley, salt and pepper. Serve the herb butter as it is, soft and in the bowl, or put it into a butter paper and form into a roll. Chill in the fridge and slice into small pieces before serving. Delicious with cooked vegetables.

Serves 4–6

CEP BUTTER SAUCE

20 g (¾ oz) dried ceps or Italian dried mushrooms
2 shallots
1–2 tbs white wine vinegar
55 ml (2 fl oz) white wine
100 ml (3½ fl oz) whipping cream
155 g (5½ oz) butter at room temperature, preferably unsalted
salt and pepper

Soak the mushrooms in a little hot water, just enough to cover them. Chop the shallots and mushrooms and place in a saucepan over a low heat with a little of the butter. Add the vinegar and white wine, bring to the boil and reduce the mixture to one-third. Stir in the cream and let the sauce cook for one minute. Add the butter bit by bit, stirring continuously, then add salt and pepper to taste.
Ideal for steamed vegetables.

Serves 4

WATERCRESS SAUCE

2 bunches watercress
200 ml (7 fl oz) olive oil
1 egg yolk
1 tbs lemon juice
1 tsp full-flavoured French mustard
salt
½ tsp finely-chopped red chilli pepper
100 ml (3½ fl oz) whipping cream
freshly-ground pepper

Boil up a large quantity of salted water.
Drop the watercress into it for 10 seconds,
then drain and cool it in iced water. Squeeze
the water out of the bunch, transfer to a
food processor and process to a purée. Add
a little of the oil and liquidize a little further.
If desired, pass the mixture through a sieve.
Make a mayonnaise from the egg yolk, the
lemon juice, the mustard and the rest of the
oil (see page 12). Add salt and chilli pepper
to taste, then mix the cress purée into the
mayonnaise. Whip the cream and carefully
fold it in. Add pepper to taste.
Serve the sauce with hot vegetables.

Serves 6–8

HERB SABAYON

1 egg
2 egg yolks
3 tbs vegetable stock
100 g (3½ oz) butter, melted
1½ tbs lemon juice
salt and freshly ground pepper
chervil and chives

Whisk the egg, egg yolks and stock in a
saucepan over a low heat. Remove from the
heat and add the butter, little by little,
whisking all the time. Add the lemon juice,
salt and pepper to taste. Chop the herbs
finely and mix them into the sauce. Whisk
up the sauce, so that it becomes frothy.
Serve with boiled or steamed vegetables,
especially asparagus.

Serves 8–10

AVOCADO AND JALAPEÑO PEPPER SAUCE

2 ripe avocados
1 tsp jalapeño pepper or fresh chilli pepper,
finely chopped
100 ml (3½ fl oz) crème fraîche
juice of ½ lime
fresh coriander
salt

Put the avocado, jalapeño or chilli pepper
and crème fraîche into a food processor or
liquidizer and process until the mixture
becomes smooth. Add the lime juice,
coriander and salt to taste.
Serve the sauce hot, as a dipping sauce for
crudités or for cooked vegetables.

Serves 4–6

WHITE ASPARAGUS

There are about 20 different types
of asparagus but the two most
common are the green and the
white. The thick white asparagus,
grown throughout Europe, is
usually cut before the bud appears
above the ground. Alternatively,
the buds are covered by a highly
fertilized sandy earth, so that they
will grow fast but remain pale.
The green asparagus grows above
the ground and has a more fibrous
flesh. Home-grown asparagus can
be bought from May to June. Eat
it lightly boiled with vinegar,
hollandaise sauce or a little butter
sauce.

STOCK: THE BASIS OF A FINE SAUCE

The recipe for a good stock departs from normal cookery practice in one important respect: instead of using young, fresh raw materials, the ripest available are chosen. This means ripe vegetables and animals which have had time to gain plenty of flavour. It is important to try to extract all the juices from these raw materials. Always leave the stock to simmer until you are sure that all the goodness has transferred to the stock. This takes at least two hours.

Bones are important in stock-making, particularly marrow bone, but don't use too many of these aromatic bones otherwise the stock will become rather 'limey'. Good bones are sometimes hard to find, as they are often cut away and discarded by the butcher. But if you give your butcher notice of your requirements, he is usually able to supply you with the bones that you need.

For a darker stock, brown a piece of meat and add that to the stock. This also produces a slightly stronger flavour. To keep the taste of the juices which you have managed to tempt out of the bones, it is important to maintain a low and even heat. Use a saucepan with a thick bottom, so that the heat will spread evenly and hold. Don't use aluminium if possible, as the metal may affect the colour of the stock and its clarity. Be cautious with your spices when making stock and only put salt in when the stock is ready, otherwise the saltiness will become too concentrated. Stocks that are to be used as a base for sauces are best left unspiced. Fresh herbs and spices can be added along with the other sauce ingredients.

As the stock heats up, it forms a froth on its surface. If you want a clear stock, you must skim this off now and again. Apart from this, a stock can be left to simmer with very little attention. When it is ready, sieve it through a wire sieve or even, if you want a very clear stock, through a fine cloth.

If the stock is not to be used straightaway leave it to cool, uncovered, then store in the fridge in a container with an airtight lid. The stock will keep in the fridge for 3 or 4 days. Alternatively, the stock, once cooled, can be transferred to a plastic, lidded container and frozen.

Here is a recipe for a meat stock which forms the basis of many brown sauces:

MEAT STOCK

1 carrot, 1 leek, 1 small onion, 1 small piece celeriac, 1 kg (2¼ lb) meat bones, ½ bay leaf, 4 peppercorns and ½ tsp salt.

1. Chop the vegetables and put them into a large saucepan together with the bones, the bay leaf and the seasoning.

2. Cover them with water.

3. Let the whole mixture simmer, uncovered, for about 2 hours, or until the stock has cooked out all the goodness and is the right consistency.

4. Remove the bones and sieve the stock and vegetables through a wire sieve.

5. Warm up the stock and use to make a sauce. Dilute with water if necessary and spice according to taste.

6. Alternatively, leave to cool, then store as directed above.

SAUCES FOR MEAT

CURRY CREAM SAUCE

½ onion, 1 banana, 1 apple, 2 pieces crystallized ginger, 2 tbs butter, 1–2 tbs mild curry powder, 285 ml (10 fl oz) whipping cream, salt and pepper.

Chop the onion, banana, apple and ginger into small pieces.

Fry the onion in butter to soften, then add the rest of the chopped ingredients.

Sprinkle curry powder on top and add the cream. Stir.

Let the sauce bubble over a low heat until it thickens. Add salt and pepper to taste. Served with fried or grilled pork.

Serves 4

ONION SAUCE

2 onions, butter, 500 ml (18 fl oz) milk, 3–4 tbs beurre manié (see page 13) and possibly half a cube of stock.

Peel and chop the onion finely. Fry slowly in the butter until it becomes soft and golden yellow.

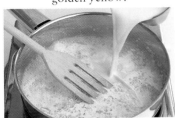

Add the milk and bring the mixture to the boil.

Add the beurre manié whilst whisking continuously and let the sauce cook for 3–5 minutes. Add the stock cube if a stronger flavour is required.
This sauce is a must with fried or grilled pork or boiled potatoes.

Serves 4

CREAM SAUCE FOR SAUTÉED MEAT

200 ml (7 fl oz) whipping cream, 100 ml (3½ fl oz) stock or water. Sauté the meat carefully, so that the juices do not burn.

When the meat is cooked, transfer to a serving dish and keep it warm.

Pour the cream and the stock or water directly into the frying pan.

Add flavourings for the sauce according to the various suggestions opposite or flavour with your own favourite spices. For a thicker sauce, whisk in 1 tbs flour mixed with a little cold water. Let the sauce cook for 3–5 minutes in order to cook the flour.

Serves 3–4

4 FLAVOURED CREAM SAUCES

Tomato Sauce: 3 tbs tomato purée, soy sauce
Blue Cheese Sauce: 55 g (2 oz) blue cheese
Mushroom Sauce: 200 g (7 oz) mushrooms
Mustard Sauce: mustard and tarragon

For the tomato sauce, add the tomato purée, the soy sauce and black pepper to taste. Bring to the boil. Good with pork chops.

For the blue cheese sauce, add the blue cheese and stir until melted. Add pepper to taste. Serve with beef and lamb fillets.

For the mushroom sauce, fry the mushrooms in a little butter. Add the cream, stock, a little soy sauce, then salt and pepper to taste. Good with all fried meats.

For the mustard sauce, add 1–2 tbs mustard and 1 tsp dried tarragon, with salt and pepper to taste.
Serve with cutlets and fillets.

Serves 3–4

PORT STEAK

approx. 1.5 kg (3¼ lb) good quality boneless steak in one piece
⅓ bottle port
50–100 ml (2–3½ fl oz) undiluted blackcurrant juice
100 ml (3½ fl oz) soy sauce
1 tsp dried thyme
5–6 juniper berries
5–6 black peppercorns
2–3 meat stock cubes
2 peeled cloves garlic
1 large onion

For the sauce you need:
800 ml (28 fl oz) meat juice
200 ml (7 fl oz) whipping cream
5 tbs flour

Choose a pan large enough to hold the meat with a thermometer. Pour in the port, blackcurrant juice and the soy sauce. Add the herbs and spices, the stock cubes, the garlic cloves, cut in two, and the onion, chopped into large pieces. Bring to the boil. Insert a meat thermometer into the thickest part of the meat. Lay the meat in the port mixture, cover and let the whole mixture simmer slowly. Turn the steak once during cooking. Take the pan off the heat when the temperature inside the meat has reached 75 °C/167 °F (about 1½ hours). Leave to rest for about 20 minutes before slicing. To make the sauce: pour the juice into a saucepan and bring to the boil. Whip together the cream and the flour. Whisk into the juice. Cook for 3–5 minutes.

Serves 12

FRUIT SAUCE

2 × 210 g (7½ oz) cans mushrooms
1 onion
1 tbs curry powder
butter
1 tbs flour
100 ml (3½ fl oz) stock
1 × 400 g (14 oz) can chopped tomatoes
1 tbs soy sauce
3 tbs concentrated frozen orange juice, thawed
200 ml (7 fl oz) crème fraîche
salt
white pepper
1 × 425 g (15 oz) can apricots

Pour the juice off the mushrooms and reserve. Peel and finely chop the onion. Fry the mushrooms, onion and curry powder gently in a little butter. Sprinkle over the flour and stir to mix. Add the stock, the reserved mushroom juice, the tomatoes, soy sauce, orange juice and the crème fraîche, stirring continuously. Bring to the boil and cook for about 10 minutes. Add salt and pepper to taste. Pour in the apricots and a little of the juice. If you want a smooth sauce, purée in a food processor.
This sauce is wonderful with all fried or grilled pork dishes.

Serves 8

1 onion, 1 tbs butter, 1–2 tbs dried, crushed pink peppercorns, 1 tbs mild mustard, 100 ml (3½ fl oz) meat juice or stock, 285 ml (10 fl oz) whipping cream, salt and pepper.

Chop the onion finely.

OLD-FASHIONED GRAVY

meat juice
whipping cream
beurre manié (see page 13)
salt and pepper

When frying a piece of meat, add a small amount of water, stock or a favourite marinade and cook together. Turn the meat in the meat juice, then add a little more liquid. After you have done this 3 or 4 times, the sauce will become delicately flavoured. Watch the sauce carefully, to ensure it doesn't burn. When the frying is finished, sieve the liquid into a measuring jug and skim off any fat that may have gathered. Dilute the meat juice with water or stock to make it up to 55 ml (2 fl oz) per serving, then increase this volume to 100 ml (3½ fl oz) per portion by adding cream. Return to the pan and cook the sauce for a few minutes, then thicken it carefully with beurre manié. Add salt and pepper to taste. If you like, you can add currant jelly, nutmeg or blue cheese as an additional flavouring.

RED PEPPER SAUCE

1 onion
2 peeled cloves garlic
½ red pepper
butter
255 ml (9 fl oz) stock
1 tbs paprika powder
½ tsp cumin
½ tsp marjoram
1–2 tbs beurre manié (see page 13)
100 ml (3½ fl oz) whipping cream
salt
100 ml (3½ fl oz) crème fraîche

Chop up the onion, the garlic and the pepper into small pieces. Fry in butter for a little while to soften, then add the stock, the spices and the marjoram. Thicken with the beurre manié and cook for 3–5 minutes. Stir in the cream and add salt to taste. The sauce may be sieved if desired or else you can run it in a liquidizer. Serve with a dollop of crème fraîche on each portion.
This is a good sauce with fricadelles.

Serves 4–5

Melt the butter and fry the onion with the peppercorns but don't let the onion brown.

Stir in the mustard, meat juice or stock and cream.

Bring to the boil, stirring continuously. Add salt and pepper to taste and you may like to add a few extra peppercorns as a garnish before serving.
This is ideal for cutlets or meatballs.

Serves 4

ORANGE SAUCE

200 ml (7 fl oz) whipping cream, 1 stock cube (vegetable stock is particularly good), 4 tbs concentrated frozen orange juice, thawed.

Pour the cream into a saucepan and bring to the boil.

Crumble in the stock cube and dissolve it in the cream.

Add the orange juice and let the sauce cook gently for 2–3 minutes, stirring frequently. Serve with fried or grilled pork of all types.

Serves 4

BLACK PEPPER SAUCE

½ onion, 1 tbs crushed black peppercorns, butter, 55 ml (2 fl oz) water, 200 ml (7 fl oz) whipping cream, 1–2 tsp freshly-squeezed lemon juice, salt. Fry the chosen meat, remove from the pan and reserve.

Chop the onion finely and fry it with the peppercorns in the butter until softened.

Add the water and bring the mixture to the boil.

Pour in the cream and let the sauce cook until thickened. Add the lemon juice and salt to taste. Return the meat to the pan to heat through.

Serves 3–4

SHERRY VINEGAR SAUCE

4 pieces of fillet steak, 3 tbs sherry vinegar, 100 ml (3½ fl oz) meat stock, 200 ml (7 fl oz) whipping cream, 2 tbs beurre manié (see page 13), salt and pepper.
Fry the steak until almost cooked then:

Pour the vinegar, stock and cream into the frying pan and cook gently for 4–5 minutes.

Transfer the pieces of meat to a warm plate. Cover with foil to keep warm.

Whisk the beurre manié into the sauce mixture. Cook for 3 minutes. Add salt and pepper to taste.

If a smooth sauce is preferred, sieve before serving. Pour the sauce over the meat.

Serves 4

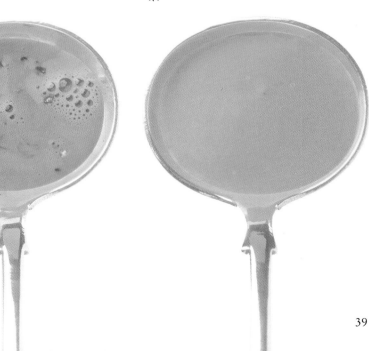

MUSTARD SAUCE

1 finely-chopped onion
2 tbs butter
200 ml (7 fl oz) dry white wine
3 tbs French mustard
285 ml (10 fl oz) whipping cream
salt and freshly ground pepper

Fry the onion in the butter without letting it brown. Add the wine and boil until almost all the liquid has evaporated. Stir in the mustard and the cream. Continue to boil until the sauce has thickened, then add salt and pepper to taste. Serve with fried or grilled meat.

Serves 4

ROSEMARY SAUCE

100 ml (3½ fl oz) meat juice or water
sprig of rosemary
285 ml (10 fl oz) whipping cream or crème fraîche
salt and freshly ground pepper
2 tbs chopped fresh parsley

Spike the chosen meat with a little rosemary. Fry the meat, then remove and keep warm. Boil the meat juice or water in the pan and add a little rosemary to taste. Boil for a few minutes, then add the cream or crème fraîche. Reduce the mixture until it begins to thicken. Add salt and pepper to taste and stir in the parsley. A perfect sauce for fried meat.

Serves 4

MUSHROOM SAUCE

55 g (2 oz) mushrooms, chopped
30 g (1 oz) dried morel mushrooms, soaked for 20 minutes
3 tbs finely-chopped shallots
2 tbs butter
55 ml (2 fl oz) white port
285 ml (10 fl oz) whipping cream
2 leaves from a savoy cabbage
salt and freshly ground pepper

Fry the mushrooms and the onion in the butter without burning. Add the port and heat through. Stir in the cream and let the sauce cook a while. Remove the stem from the cabbage leaves and cut the leaves into broad strips. Add these strips just before serving. Bring the sauce to the boil once more, then add salt and pepper to taste. Serve with fried or grilled meat, particularly lamb.

Serves 3–4

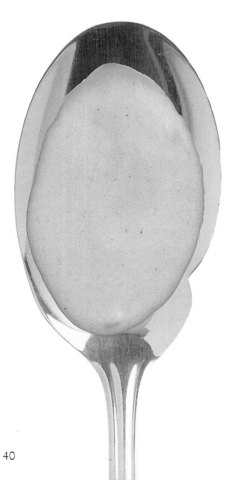

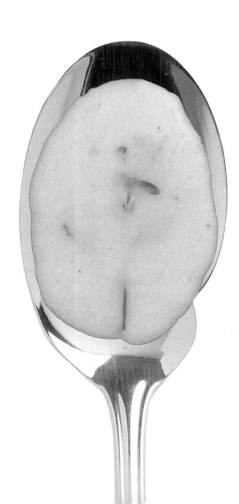

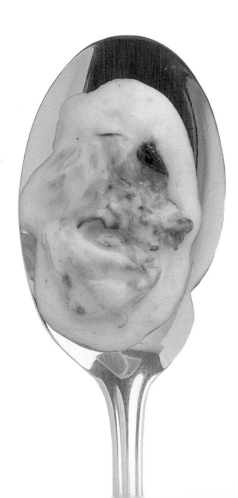

BLUE CHEESE SAUCE WITH SHERRY

1 finely-chopped onion
2 tbs butter
55 g (2 oz) blue cheese
1 tbs mustard
100 ml (3½ fl oz) medium-dry sherry
285 ml (10 fl oz) single cream
salt and pepper

Fry the onion in the butter without browning. Crumble most of the blue cheese into the mixture, then add the mustard and sherry. Stir well. Bring to the boil, then add the cream. Let the sauce cook a little while longer, then add salt and pepper to taste. Crumble the rest of the cheese into the sauce just before serving.
Delicious with fried or grilled meat, particularly liver.

Serves 4–6

TOMATO SAUCE

200 g (7 oz) butter
1 tbs fresh thyme
1 tbs fresh sage
1 tbs fresh tarragon
1 peeled clove garlic
2 tbs tomato purée
100–140 ml (3½–5 fl oz) stock, preferably lamb stock
salt and freshly-ground pepper

Put the butter, thyme, sage, tarragon, garlic and tomato purée into a food processor and purée. Bring the stock to the boil, then lower the heat and add the butter mixture gradually. Whisk continuously and do not let the sauce boil. Add salt and pepper to taste. Sieve the mixture if preferred.
This is very good with any lamb dish.

Serves 4–6

FLAMBÉ SAUCE

100 ml (3½ fl oz) whipping cream
2 tbs cognac
2 tbs mustard
1 tsp freshly-squeezed lemon juice
salt and freshly-ground pepper
meat juice if available

Whip the cream. Pour the cognac into a warmed pan and light it. Have a lid ready just in case the fire gets out of control. When the flame has extinguished itself, pour in the whipped cream. Add the mustard and stir thoroughly. Add the lemon juice, salt and pepper to taste. If you have meat juice, pour it into the sauce at this point and warm the mixture over a high heat for 1–2 minutes.
This is good with fried or grilled meats, particularly fillets.

Serves 2

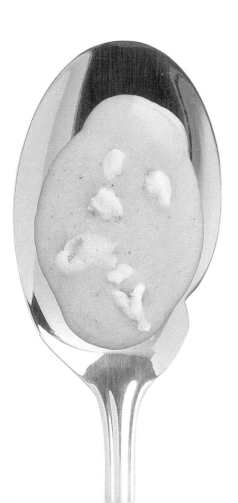
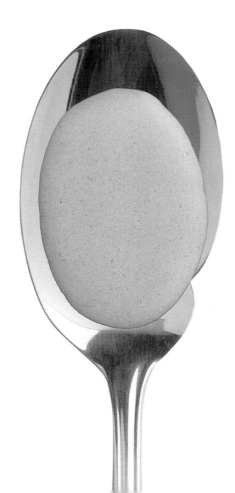
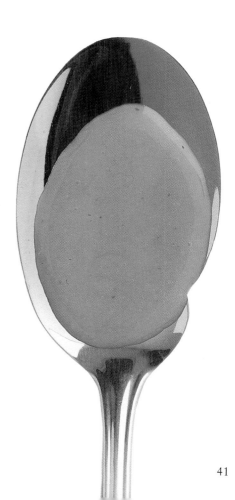

ITALIAN SAUCE

1 leek, butter, 1 × 400 g (14 oz) can chopped tomatoes, 200 ml (7 fl oz) whipping cream, 2 tbs tomato purée, 1 squeezed clove garlic, 1 tsp dried oregano, salt, white pepper, juice of ½ lemon.

Shred the leek and fry it gently in the butter.

Drain the liquid from the tomatoes and pour them into the saucepan.

Add the cream, the tomato purée, garlic, oregano, seasoning and lemon juice. Stir well and cook for a few minutes. This sauce is ideal for adding interest to chops and other pork dishes.

Serves 6

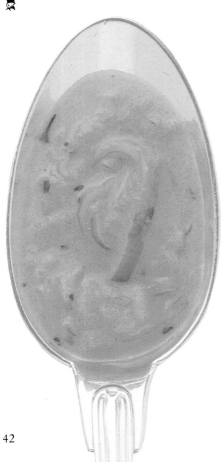

HERB SPICED SAUCE

3 tbs butter, 3 tbs flour, 285 ml (10 fl oz) meat stock, 200 ml (7 fl oz) whipping cream, 4 tbs finely-chopped fresh parsley, 1 tsp dried chervil, 1 tsp dried tarragon, salt and pepper, soy sauce.

Melt the butter, add the flour and stir thoroughly. Cook for 1–2 minutes.

Stir in the meat stock and the cream gradually, then cook for about 5 minutes.

Stir in the parsley, chervil and tarragon. Add salt, pepper and soy sauce to taste. This sauce is tasty with fried and grilled meat and chicken.

Serves 4–6

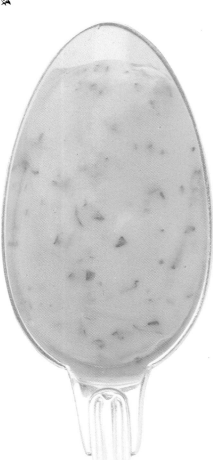

CAPER SAUCE

285 ml (10 fl oz) meat juice or meat stock, 100 ml (3½ fl oz) whipping cream or crème fraîche, 3–4 tbs beurre manié (see page 13), 2 mashed fillets of sardines, 2 tbs capers.

Pour the stock and the cream or crème fraîche into a saucepan and bring to the boil.

Whisk in the beurre manié and let the sauce cook for 3–5 minutes.

Stir in the mashed sardines and the capers and heat through. This sauce is good with roast meat and fricadelles.

Serves 4–6

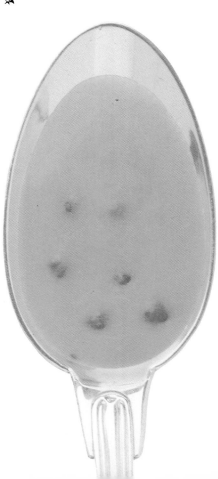

MUSHROOM AND PORT SAUCE

2 shallots, 200 g (7 oz) mushrooms, butter, 1–2 tbs red port, 100 ml (3½ fl oz) stock, 200 ml (7 fl oz) whipping cream or crème fraîche, salt and pepper.

Peel and chop the onion finely and slice the mushrooms.

Fry the onions in the butter over a low heat until softened but not browned. Add the mushrooms.

Pour in the wine and let the sauce cook for a few minutes.

Pour in the stock and the cream or crème fraîche and cook the sauce for a further 5 minutes. Add salt and pepper to taste. Serve with fried or grilled meat.

Serves 3–4

GAME SAUCE

285 ml (10 fl oz) meat juice from hare or venison or game stock
285 ml (10 fl oz) single cream
salt
white pepper
8–10 juniper berries
2–3 tbs redcurrant jelly
3–4 tbs beurre manié (see page 13)

Mix the meat juice or the stock and the cream in a saucepan. Cook uncovered for 5–10 minutes. Add the salt, white pepper, juniper berries and jelly to taste. Whisk in the beurre manié bit by bit. Cook over a medium heat for 3–5 minutes.
Beautiful with hare, venison and other game meat.

Serves 6

CREAMY MINT SAUCE

3 tbs butter
3 tbs flour
500 ml (about 18 fl oz) milk
1 tbs dried mint or 2–3 tbs fresh mint, chopped
1 tsp salt
¼ tsp white pepper

Melt the butter. Mix in the flour and cook for 1–2 minutes, stirring constantly. Add the milk gradually, whisking all the time. Let the sauce cook for 3–5 minutes. Sprinkle the mint into the sauce. Season with salt and pepper and serve with all types of lamb, roast, grilled or fried.

Serves 4–6

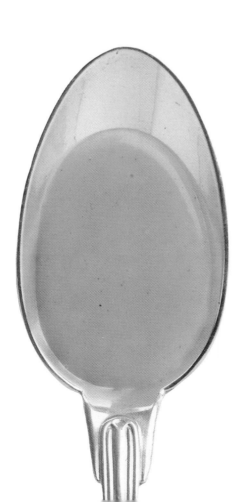

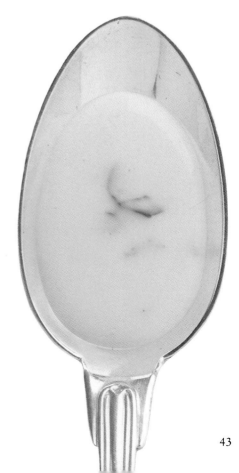

BLUE CHEESE SAUCE

2 tbs butter, 2 tbs flour, 500 ml (about 18 fl oz) milk, 55 g (2 oz) blue cheese, ½ tsp salt, ¼ tsp white pepper, 2 tsp cream or crème fraîche.

Melt the butter, then stir in the flour and cook for 1–2 minutes.

Add the milk gradually. Whisk thoroughly, bring to the boil and cook for 5 minutes.

Crumble the blue cheese into the sauce and add salt and pepper to taste.

Stir until the cheese has melted, then add the cream or crème fraîche.
Serve with fried or grilled meat, particularly with beef.

Serves 4–5

HORSERADISH SAUCE

200 ml (7 fl oz) meat stock or meat juice, 285 ml (10 fl oz) milk, 3–4 tbs beurre manié (see page 13), 2 tbs grated horseradish, few drops of vinegar, ½ tsp sugar.

Pour the stock and the milk into a saucepan and bring to the boil.

Whisk in the beurre manié. Let the sauce cook for 3–5 minutes.

Add the horseradish, vinegar and sugar to taste.
This sauce is ideal with all roast meats.

Serves 4

DILL SAUCE

3 tbs butter, 3 tbs flour, ¼ tsp white pepper, 500 ml (about 18 fl oz) meat juice or stock, ½ tsp sugar, ½ tbs white vinegar, salt if desired, 3 tbs finely-chopped fresh dill, 55 ml (2 fl oz) whipping cream.

Melt the butter, adding the flour and white pepper as you stir. Cook for 1–2 minutes.

Stir in the meat juice or stock gradually and whisk thoroughly.

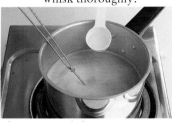

Let the sauce cook for 5–10 minutes. Add the sugar, vinegar and salt to taste.

Stir in the dill and cream and serve with cooked meat, lamb, veal or pork. Also good with chicken.

Serves 4

BÉARNAISE SAUCE

155 g (5½ oz) butter, 1 tbs finely-chopped shallots or onion, 4 crushed white peppercorns, 2 tbs vinegar, 4 tbs water, 2 egg yolks, 2 tbs finely-chopped fresh parsley, 1–2 tbs finely-chopped fresh tarragon (or 1–2 tsp dried, crushed).

Melt the butter in a saucepan and set aside.

Put the onion, peppercorns, vinegar and 2 tbs of the water in another pan and boil.

When the liquid has almost boiled away, add 2 more tbs of water. Strain to remove onion if desired. Put the saucepan into a bain marie, i.e. into a larger saucepan containing hot water. The water should not boil. Add the egg yolks and whisk gently.

Whisk in the melted butter little by little. Add the parsley and the tarragon to taste. Delicious with roast fillet of beef.

Serves 4–6

HUNTSMAN'S CASSEROLE

100 ml (3½ fl oz) stock, 100 ml (3½ fl oz) red wine, 2 tbs soy sauce, 8–10 juniper berries, ½ tsp allspice, ¼ tsp black pepper, ¼ tsp ground cloves, 1 bay leaf, 400 g (14 oz) beef or pork steak, cut in strips, 200 ml (7 fl oz) whipping cream.

Place the stock, wine, soy sauce and spices in a saucepan and bring to the boil.

Add the strips of meat. Simmer, covered, until tender, 30–45 minutes.

Add the cream and let the mixture cook for another 10 minutes.
Serve with rice, potatoes or pasta.

Serves 4

PARSLEY BUTTER

6 tbs fresh parsley, 100 g (3½ oz) butter at room temperature, few drops of freshly-squeezed lemon juice, ½–1 tsp freshly-ground white pepper and a few drops Worcestershire sauce.

Chop the parsley very finely and mix together thoroughly with the butter.

Stir in the lemon juice, pepper and Worcestershire sauce to taste.

HORSERADISH BUTTER

100 g (3½ oz) butter at room temperature, 1–2 tbs finely-grated horseradish, few drops of vinegar, ½ tsp sugar.

Mix all the ingredients together and serve at room temperature. Ideal for beef.

Herb butters are best served at room temperature, so that they will melt quickly on hot meats.

Serves 5–6

GARLIC SAUCE

310 g (11 oz) garlic (6–7 whole garlics)
200 ml (7 fl oz) single cream
200 ml (7 fl oz) milk
200 ml (7 fl oz) meat juice from lamb, or stock
1–2 tbs beurre manié (see page 13), if necessary
1 tsp salt
juice of ½–1 lemon

Peel the garlic cloves and cook in the milk and the cream in a covered saucepan over a gentle heat until they become mushy (15–30 minutes). Liquidize the garlic and the cream mixture, then pour back into the saucepan. Add the stock and the beurre manié if desired. Let the sauce cook for 3–5 minutes. Add salt and lemon juice to taste.
This is a fantastic sauce for fried or grilled meat, especially lamb.

Serves 6–8

WHITE WINE AND HERB SAUCE

1 finely-chopped onion
3 tbs unsalted butter
1 tsp finely-chopped fresh parsley
1 tsp chervil, fresh if possible
1 tsp tarragon, fresh if possible
1 tsp finely-chopped chives
1 tbs tomato purée
100 ml (3½ fl oz) meat stock
100 ml (3½ fl oz) dry white wine
285 ml (10 fl oz) whipping cream
3 tbs beurre manié (see page 13)
salt and freshly-ground pepper
100 g (3½ oz) finely-chopped cucumber

Fry the onion in 1 tbs of the butter until softened. Add the green herbs and tomato purée. Pour in the stock and the wine and bring the mixture to the boil. Add the cream and let the whole mixture cook for 10–15 minutes. Whisk in the beurre manié bit by bit. Let the sauce cook for a few minutes longer, then add salt and pepper to taste. Mix in the cucumber and heat through. Add remaining 2 tbs unsalted butter off the heat and stir until the sauce becomes glossy. Ideal for fried or grilled meat.

Serves 6

CIDER SAUCE

4 portions rabbit
155 g (5½ oz) butter
6–8 finely-chopped shallots
sprig fresh thyme
salt and freshly-ground pepper
55 ml (2 fl oz) calvados
500 ml (about 18 fl oz) dry cider
3 cooking apples

Cook the rabbit in the butter in a covered, flameproof casserole until the meat is brown all over. Add the shallots and the thyme and simmer, covered, until the onions are soft but not browned. Season with salt and pepper. Pour over the calvados, ignite carefully and flambé the mixture. Add the cider when the flame has burnt out and simmer, uncovered, until the meat is tender, about 40 minutes, depending on size. Meanwhile, peel the apples, core them and cut into quarters. Fry them gently in a little butter. When the rabbit is cooked, transfer to a serving dish and sieve cooking liquor into a saucepan. Whisk in the butter, bit by bit, then heat through. Add the apples and pour the sauce over the meat.

Serves 4

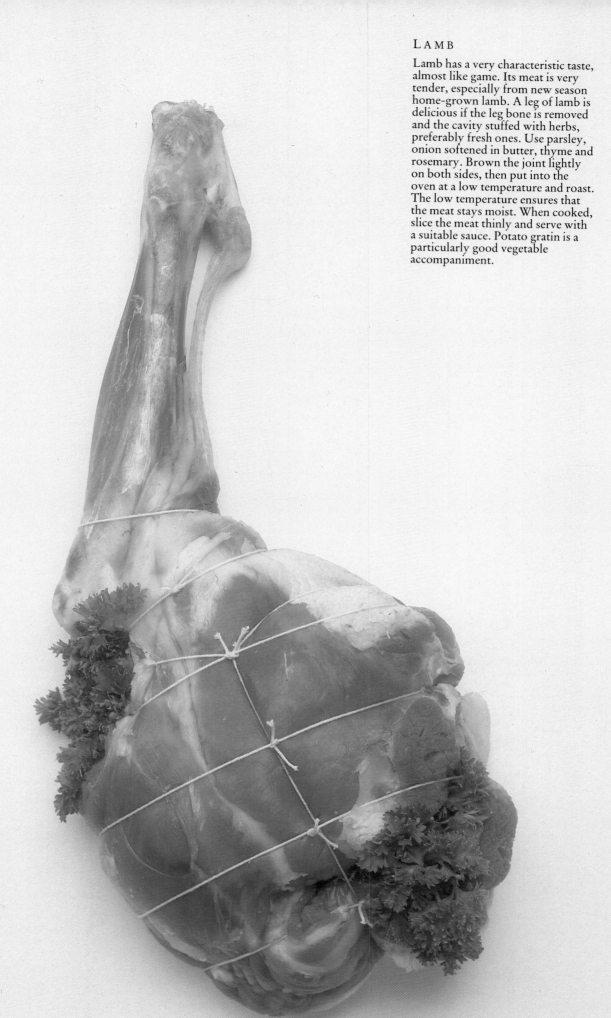

LAMB

Lamb has a very characteristic taste, almost like game. Its meat is very tender, especially from new season home-grown lamb. A leg of lamb is delicious if the leg bone is removed and the cavity stuffed with herbs, preferably fresh ones. Use parsley, onion softened in butter, thyme and rosemary. Brown the joint lightly on both sides, then put into the oven at a low temperature and roast. The low temperature ensures that the meat stays moist. When cooked, slice the meat thinly and serve with a suitable sauce. Potato gratin is a particularly good vegetable accompaniment.

GREEN HERB SAUCE

30 g (1 oz) chives
30 g (1 oz) fresh parsley
15 g (½ oz) fresh tarragon
85 g (3 oz) spinach
400 g (14 oz) butter at room temperature
155 ml (5½ fl oz) meat stock
½ tsp aniseed
½ tsp fennel seeds
salt and freshly-ground pepper

Put the chives, parsley, tarragon and
spinach into a food processor or liquidizer.
Add the butter and process. Boil the stock,
aniseed and fennel together until reduced by
half. Sieve the stock into a clean saucepan,
then whisk in the herb butter, bit by bit. Do
not let the stock boil. Add salt and pepper
to taste and serve with fried or grilled meat,
especially veal.

Serves 6–8

CAFÉ DE PARIS SAUCE

3 sardines
1 tbs tomato ketchup
1½ tsp Dijon mustard
1 tbs capers
2 shallots
6 tbs finely-chopped fresh parsley
3 tbs finely-chopped chives
1 tbs finely-chopped fresh dill
1 tsp fresh thyme
1 tsp dried tarragon
1 tsp fresh rosemary
1 peeled clove garlic
1 tsp cognac
1 tsp medium-dry madeira
½ tsp Worcestershire sauce
3 white peppercorns
½ tsp paprika powder
¼ green pepper
½ tsp curry powder
pinch cayenne pepper
juice of ¼ lemon
grated peel of ⅛ lemon
¼ tsp grated orange peel
310 g (11 oz) butter at room temperature

Put all the ingredients except for the butter
into a food processor and process until the
mixture becomes smooth. If it is too thick,
add a few drops of sardine oil or another oil
Let the mixture stand for a day. Next day,
stir the butter and mix it into the herb
mixture. Serve this herb butter either soft or
place in a butter paper and roll into a
sausage shape, which you can put into the
fridge, then slice off portions as needed.
Serve with roast and grilled meats of all
kinds.

Serves 15–20

VEAL

Veal is most plentiful in the summer. The meat from very young animals has a very mild flavour. For a spicier taste, make a bundle of herbs and add to the veal joint when you cook it. Roll some thyme, rosemary, mint, tarragon and parsley together in a leaf of celery or leek and bind with string. A mushroom sauce or a sauce made with fresh herbs are ideal with veal dishes.

SAUCES – A CORNERSTONE OF COOKING

With its origins in the 16th century and well established a century later, French cuisine has gained world renown and has often been described as the very mother of the art of cooking. Its influence on cooking and gastronomy the world over has been immense and there are many who believe that the sauces themselves have been the crucial factor in this reputation. There are hundreds of French sauces, many of which have become classics.

Marie-Antoine Carême (1784–1833) – one of France's greatest gastronomic figures and seen as the founder of *la grande cuisine*, the epitome of his country's cooking – developed many of these classics. He recognized that sauces were a major factor in his country's culinary identity and capitalized on the change in texture and flavour which sauces were then undergoing: from coarse and thin to smooth and velvety. He classified sauces into four families, with one leading sauce in each, to which numerous different flavourings and seasonings could be added.

His successor, Auguste Escoffier (1846–1935), built on and refined Carême's system to name five leading or mother sauces: espagnole (brown); velouté (light); béchamel (white); tomato and hollandaise. His ground rules are still relevant today. It was mainly through Escoffier that French cuisine spread across the world, not least through his collaboration with the famous international hotelier, César Ritz.

France is, of course, not the sole source of good sauces: Italy, for example, has a distinguished array of sauces which make a substantial contribution to its fine cuisine. The emphasis is on vegetable purées, especially tomato, and simple olive oil and wine mixtures. Hannah Glasse, whose 18th century English cookbooks gained her great popularity, has a gravy as her principal sauce, made by browning meat with carrots and onions, adding herbs and spices and cooking together in water until all the flavours are released. Modern British cooking still places great store by the art of gravy making.

A sauce makes or breaks a meal. In high-class restaurants there will be a particular cook responsible for all the sauces. Called *le saucier* he is next in rank to the master chef and therefore a person of great skill and long experience in this field. His is a highly important task, since the greatest qualities of an individual cuisine are united in a good sauce: it is proof of the cook's creativity and skill.

But the most important part depends on a practised palate making the right decision. This art cannot be learned either from books or by instruction: only by experience and conscientious practice.

A sauce should be tasted at various stages during its preparation but particularly before and during the addition of seasonings and flavourings. A savoury sauce can be spoiled just by adding too much salt (see page 100 for advice on this aspect) and it is equally important to be careful with the sugar in a sweet sauce. Sauces that contain acid in the form of wine, vinegar or lemon juice should be carefully balanced in their acidity, whilst fat-based sauces, such as béarnaise, hollandaise or mayonnaise, are tasteless without a fresh and slightly sharp flavouring. Alain Chapel, the renowned French master chef, allows no seasonings on the tables of his Lyons restaurant, since he maintains that the meals have all been perfectly balanced and need nothing further!

A good home-made sauce is far superior to commercially-available alternatives, so don't be afraid of failing to begin with. You will learn by your mistakes and gradually a pattern will emerge which will give you the confidence to expand and experiment to develop your own repertoire.

SAUCES FOR POULTRY AND GAME

CHICKEN LIVER SAUCE

1 crushed clove garlic, 2 tbs concentrated frozen orange juice, thawed, 6 tbs finely-chopped fresh parsley, ¼ tsp black pepper, 200 ml (7 fl oz) whipping cream, 400 g (14 oz) chicken livers, butter, ½ tsp salt.

Mix the garlic, orange juice, parsley, pepper and cream. Transfer to a saucepan and cook the mixture for 2–3 minutes.

Slice the livers into pieces and fry slowly in butter for about 5 minutes.

Add the pieces of liver to the sauce and heat through. Add salt to taste.
Serve with rice or potatoes.

Serves 4

PINEAPPLE SAUCE

½ can crushed pineapple (about 325 g (11½ oz), 200 ml (7 fl oz) sour cream, 1–2 tsp mustard.

Drain the juice carefully from the pineapple.

Mix the sour cream and the mustard in a serving bowl.

Stir in the pineapple.
This sauce is good for chicken salad or smoked chicken.

Serves 4

HORSERADISH APPLE SAUCE

200 ml (7 fl oz) apple sauce, 200 ml (7 fl oz) sour cream, juice of ½ lemon, 2–3 tbs grated horseradish.

Mix together the apple sauce and the sour cream.

Add lemon juice to taste.

Add the grated horseradish and stir.
Serve with chicken or turkey, warm or cold.

Serves 4

CURRY CREAM SAUCE

1 finely-chopped, peeled clove garlic, ½ tbs curry powder, 1–2 tbs butter, 1 tbs tomato ketchup, 200 ml (7 fl oz) crème fraîche, 155 ml (5½ fl oz) whipping cream.

Fry the finely-chopped garlic with the curry powder in the butter.

Take the saucepan off the heat and mix in the tomato ketchup.

Add the crème fraîche.

Whip the cream and fold it into the crème fraîche mixture.
Serve with cold chicken.

Serves·6

CURRY SAUCE

about 100 g (3½ oz) desiccated coconut
1 chicken, weighing about 1 kg (2¼ lb)
5 cloves garlic, peeled and chopped
1 large onion, peeled and chopped
1 large potato, peeled
100 g (3½ oz) butter
1 cinnamon stick
1 tsp curry powder
1 red pepper
cayenne pepper

Put the desiccated coconut into a bowl and pour over enough boiling water just to cover. Leave the coconut to stand and infuse. Cut the chicken into 8–10 pieces. Cut up the potato. Fry the garlic and onion with the cinnamon stick and the curry powder in half of the butter in a large saucepan. Put the potato and chicken pieces into the saucepan and add 200 ml (7 fl oz) water. Bring to the boil, cover and cook for 20 minutes. Prepare the pepper and slice it into large pieces. Add it to the saucepan and cook for another 20 minutes. When the chicken is ready, the casserole should have a slightly porridgy consistency. Pour the coconut into a sieve over a basin and press out the coconut milk. Stir the coconut milk into the casserole and add the rest of the butter bit by bit, stirring constantly. Let this mixture boil as you stir it. Add cayenne pepper to taste. Serve with boiled rice. You could also serve small side dishes of sour cream, mango chutney, sliced cucumber and banana, slices of pepper, peanuts and the desiccated coconut.

Serves 4

GRAVY FOR GAME

1 game bird
100 ml (3½ fl oz) stock
½ bay leaf
½ tsp thyme
285 ml (10 fl oz) whipping cream
2 tsp cognac

Fry the fowl slowly until just cooked, then let it rest for 5–10 minutes before cutting out every bone except for the thigh bone. Skin the breast and keep warm with the thighs. Discard the pelvic bone, that is the bone nearest the rump, as this has a bitter taste. All the other bones and the rest of the skin should be cooked in the stock with the spices. Add the cream and let that boil up with the bones until the mixture becomes thick. Sieve well, shaking and pressing all the sauce through the sieve. Add a few drops of cognac to taste.

Serves 4

TARRAGON HERB SAUCE

400 ml (14 fl oz) chicken stock
6 tbs beurre manié (see page 13)
2 egg yolks
200 ml (7 fl oz) crème fraîche
30 g (1 oz) butter at room temperature
2 tbs chopped fresh tarragon or
1 tbs dried tarragon
salt and pepper

Sieve the stock into a saucepan and skim off
any fat. Bring to the boil and continue to
boil until reduced by half. Thicken it
carefully with beurre manié until desired
consistency is reached. Mix the egg yolks
with the crème fraîche in a bowl. Carefully
pour the hot sauce into the bowl while
whisking thoroughly, then pour the sauce
back into the saucepan and whisk in the
butter over a gentle heat. Do not let the
sauce boil again. Stir in the tarragon and add
salt and pepper to taste.
Serve with chicken pieces.

Serves 4–6

SUPREME SAUCE

400 ml (14 fl oz) chicken stock
beurre manié (see page 13)
2 egg yolks
200 ml (7 fl oz) crème fraîche
cayenne pepper
55 g (2 oz) butter

Make this sauce exactly like the Tarragon
Herb Sauce. Include vegetables when
cooking the stock and if desired, add a clove
of garlic. For a stronger flavour, add a herb
bundle containing leek, thyme, bay leaf and
parsley.
Serve with chicken pieces.

Serves 4–6

CHERRY SAUCE

1 × 210 g (7½ oz) can cherries
2 tbs butter
500 ml (about 18 fl oz) meat stock
100 g (3½ oz) butter
salt and freshly-ground white pepper

Pour off the juice from the cherries and
reserve. Fry the cherries with the butter in a
frying pan over a gentle heat. Add the stock
and cook for about 10 minutes. Push the
cherries and the liquid through a sieve or
purée them in a food processor or a
liquidizer. Return to the saucepan and bring
back to the boil, then whisk in the butter bit
by bit. Add the reserved juice from the
cherries if desired. Add salt and pepper to
taste and warm the mixture carefully. You
can also make this sauce with fresh cherries,
in which case, add 1 tsp caster sugar.
Serve this sauce with fried or grilled
poultry.

Serves 6

PARSLEY GRAVY

200 ml (7 fl oz) water, 100 g (3½ oz) butter at room temperature, 6 tbs finely-chopped fresh parsley, black pepper.
Fry some chicken pieces until just cooked, remove and keep warm.

Add water to the pan and whisk it up.

Sieve this mixture into a heavy-bottomed saucepan and skim off any fat. Reduce until about 100 ml (3½ fl oz) remains.

Whisk in the butter bit by bit. Stir in the parsley and add pepper to taste.
Serve with the reserved poultry.

Serves 4

CHICKEN GRAVY

1 chicken, 300–400 ml (11–14 fl oz) water, 8–10 sprigs parsley, 1 chopped shallot, 2 tbs beurre manié (see page 13), 200 ml (7 fl oz) whipping cream, blackcurrant jelly.
Roast the chicken, rest it for 5–10 minutes, then remove all bones except the thigh.

Boil the bones in the water with the parsley sprigs, the shallot, and if desired the giblets and the neck. Boil for about 10 minutes.

Sieve the stock into a frying pan and boil rapidly until reduced to about 155 ml (5½ fl oz).

Whisk in the beurre manié bit by bit, then stir in the cream. Let the sauce cook for 3–5 minutes. Add the blackcurrant jelly to taste.

Serves 4–6

LEMON SAUCE

2 tbs butter
2 tbs flour
400 ml (14 fl oz) chicken stock
juice of ½ lemon
200 ml (7 fl oz) whipping cream
2 tbs unsalted butter
freshly-ground salt and pepper

Melt the butter, add the flour and cook for 1–2 minutes. Add the chicken stock gradually and bring to the boil. Stir in the lemon juice and the cream and cook the whole mixture for a little while. Whisk in the butter bit by bit. Sieve the sauce and add salt and pepper to taste.
Delightful with roast chicken.

Serves 4

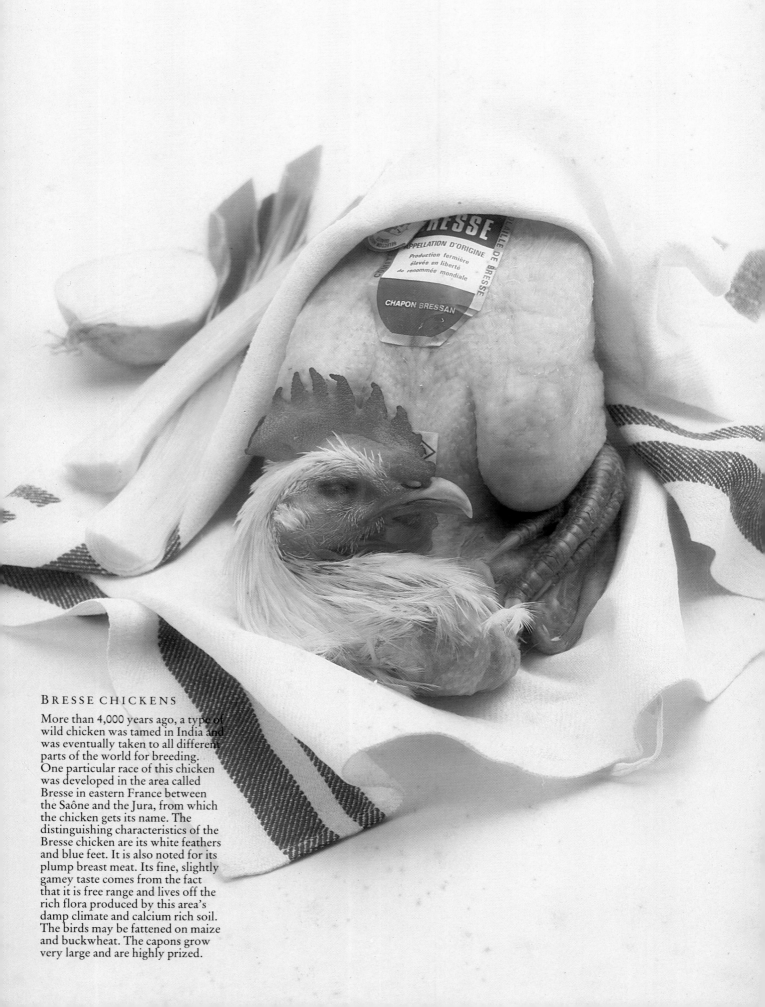

BRESSE CHICKENS

More than 4,000 years ago, a type of
wild chicken was tamed in India and
was eventually taken to all different
parts of the world for breeding.
One particular race of this chicken
was developed in the area called
Bresse in eastern France between
the Saône and the Jura, from which
the chicken gets its name. The
distinguishing characteristics of the
Bresse chicken are its white feathers
and blue feet. It is also noted for its
plump breast meat. Its fine, slightly
gamey taste comes from the fact
that it is free range and lives off the
rich flora produced by this area's
damp climate and calcium rich soil.
The birds may be fattened on maize
and buckwheat. The capons grow
very large and are highly prized.

LIME SAUCE

500 ml (about 18 fl oz) poultry stock
peel and juice from 2 limes
55 g (2 oz) unsalted butter
salt and freshly-ground pepper

Boil up the stock until it is reduced to half
its quantity. Remove the peel from the limes
with a potato peeler making sure you do not
include any of the pith. Slice the peel into
very fine strips. Whisk the butter into the
stock bit by bit, then stir in the lime juice.
Add salt and pepper to taste and garnish
with the lime strips.
Delicious with duck.

Serves 4

MUSHROOM SAUCE À LA CRÈME

200 ml (7 fl oz) chicken stock
200 ml (7 fl oz) whipping cream
55 g (2 oz) unsalted butter
255 g (9 oz) mixed mushrooms, particularly
morels and field mushrooms
1 tbs finely-chopped shallot
freshly-ground salt and white pepper

Boil up the chicken stock and the cream
together until reduced by half. Mix in the
butter. Dry-roast the mushrooms and the
shallot in a pan without any fat. Season the
mushrooms with salt and pepper. Mix the
mushrooms into the sauce just before
serving. Add salt and pepper to taste.
Ideal for roast chicken, pigeon or other
small birds.

Serves 4

PRUNE SAUCE

400 ml (14 fl oz) turkey stock
55–85 ml (2–3 fl oz) mild red wine vinegar
10 stoned prunes
½–1 finely-chopped red chilli
55 g (2 oz) unsalted butter
freshly-ground salt and pepper

Put the stock, the vinegar, the prunes and
the chilli into a saucepan, bring to the boil
and continue boiling until reduced by half.
Transfer the sauce to a food processor or
liquidizer and process, adding the butter bit
by bit. Add salt and pepper to taste. If
desired, you can warm the sauce before
serving but do so carefully.
This sauce is ideal for roast turkey.

Serves 4

SAUCES FOR FISH

SIMPLE FISH SAUCE

680 g (1½ lb) perch fillets, butter, 1 tsp salt, 200 ml (7 fl oz) crème fraîche, 1 tbs flour, ¼ tsp black pepper, 100 ml (3½ fl oz) fish stock, 1 tsp thyme, if desired.

Put the fish fillets into an ovenproof dish, sprinkle with ½ tsp of the salt, cover and bake at 200 °C/400 °F/Gas Mark 6 for 25–30 minutes. Strain off the cooking liquor.

Stir together the flour, remaining salt, pepper and crème fraîche in a saucepan.

Bring to the boil and add the fish juice. Let the sauce cook over a medium heat for 5–10 minutes. Add the thyme if desired, then pour the sauce over the fish.

Serves 4

PLAICE IN WINE SAUCE

680 g (1½ lb) plaice fillets, 55 ml (2 fl oz) fish stock, 55 ml (2½ fl oz) white wine, 1 tsp salt, ¼ tsp white pepper, 200 ml (7 fl oz) crème fraîche.

Preheat the oven to 220 °C/425 °F/Gas Mark 7. Roll up the fillets and lay them in an ovenproof dish.

Mix together the fish stock, wine, salt, pepper and crème fraîche in a bowl.

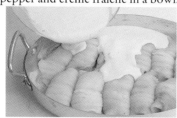

Pour this sauce over the fish, cover and bake for about 25 minutes.
Serve with potatoes and vegetables.

Serves 4

SIMPLE LOBSTER SAUCE

1 × 310 ml (11 fl oz) can lobster soup, 200 ml (7 fl oz) whipping cream or crème fraîche, 1–2 tbs cognac.

Pour the lobster soup into a saucepan and add the cream or crème fraîche.

Bring to the boil and simmer for 2–3 minutes.

Stir in the cognac. This is particularly delicious with steamed fish. It can also be used as a gratin sauce, in which case you would thicken the sauce with 3–4 tbs beurre manié (see page 13).

Serves 6

INDIAN SAUCE

1 red pepper, chopped, 1 tbs mango chutney, 1 tbs tomato ketchup, 200 ml (7 fl oz) crème fraîche or sour cream, 1 tbs curry powder.

Put the pepper, chutney and ketchup into a food processor.

Add the crème fraîche or the sour cream.

Spice with the curry powder and process until the sauce is smooth.
This sauce is particularly good with fried fish.

Serves 4

TARTAR SAUCE

200 ml (7 fl oz) crème fraîche or sour cream, 6 tbs roughly-chopped chives, 1–2 tbs pickle, 5 peeled shallots, 100 ml (3½ fl oz) whipping cream, 1 tbs mild mustard.

Put the crème fraîche or sour cream, the chives, pickle and the shallots into a food processor.

Add the whipping cream.

Add the mustard and process to a purée.
Ideal for fried or grilled fish.

Serves 6

APPLE SAUCE

1 red apple, 285 ml (10 fl oz) sour cream, 3 tbs sweet cucumber pickle.

Core the apple and slice it coarsely. Put the apple and the sour cream into a food processor.

Add the sweet pickle and process until the sauce is smooth.
This is good for fish fingers and other fried fish.

Serves 4–6

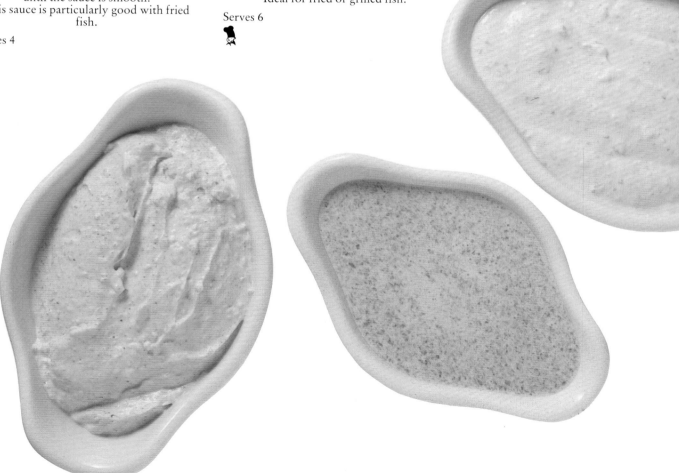

GREEN SAUCE

100 g (3½ oz) chopped, fresh spinach, 1 tbs chopped chives, 2 tbs chopped fresh parsley, 1 tbs mild mustard, 1 peeled clove garlic, 200 ml (7 fl oz) crème fraîche or sour cream, and pepper, if desired.

Put the spinach, chives, parsley and mustard into a food processor.

Add the garlic and the crème fraîche or sour cream and process until the sauce is smooth.
Add pepper to taste.
Ideal with fried and grilled fish.

Serves 4

PICKLE SAUCE

1 tbs pickle, 1 peeled shallot, 1 tbs mild mustard, 1 tsp capers, 155 ml (5½ fl oz) sour cream, 155 ml (5½ fl oz) crème fraîche, ½ tsp salt.

Put the pickle, onion, mustard and capers into a food processor.

Add the sour cream and crème fraîche.

Add salt to taste and process until the sauce is smooth. Serve with fried fish.

Serves 6

CREAMY VEGETABLE SAUCE

1 leek
1 carrot
1 onion
200 ml (7 fl oz) vegetable stock
200 ml (7 fl oz) crème fraîche
salt and pepper
tarragon, if desired

Peel and slice the vegetables. Cook them in the stock until just tender, 10–15 minutes. Put the vegetables and the stock into a food processor and liquidize. Add the crème fraîche and run the machine for another few seconds. Pour the sauce into a saucepan and add salt and pepper to taste. Add tarragon if desired, then warm the sauce carefully. This is an ideal sauce for all kinds of poached or steamed fish.

Serves 6

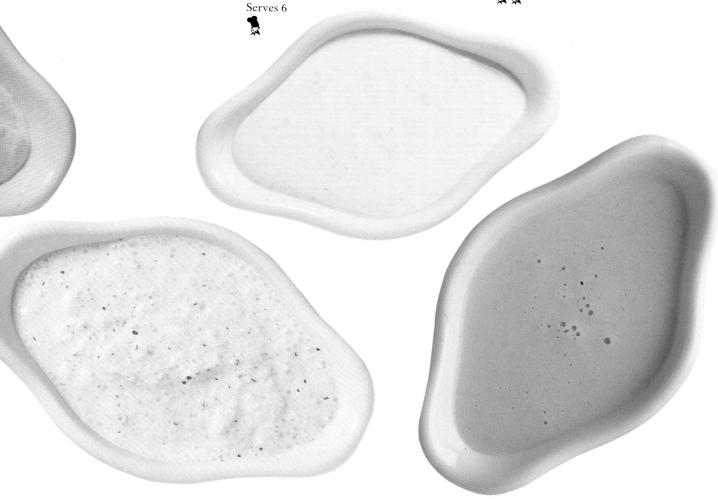

HORSERADISH À LA CRÈME

200 ml (7 fl oz) whipping cream
100 ml (3½ fl oz) fromage blanc or frais
2–3 tbs grated fresh horseradish
1–2 tbs finely-sliced chives
freshly-ground salt and pepper

Boil the cream until it is reduced to half its quantity. Cool slightly, then whisk in the fromage blanc or frais together with the other ingredients. Add salt and pepper to taste.
Serve this sauce warm or cold with salt cod. It is also very good with smoked fish.

Serves 2–3

MELTED BUTTER WITH EGG AND HORSERADISH

110 g (4 oz) butter
4 hard-boiled eggs
1 tbs fresh dill
1 tbs fresh parsley
1 tbs chives
55 g (2 oz) grated fresh horseradish or to taste
freshly-ground salt and pepper

Melt the butter. Chop up the egg, dill, parsley and chives. Mix these ingredients with the butter. Add horseradish, salt and pepper to taste.
Serve with poached cod.

Serves 4–6

GREEN SAUCE WITH CREAM CHEESE

225 g (8 oz) low fat cream cheese, e.g. cottage cheese
55 ml (2 fl oz) crème fraîche
1 tbs mild French mustard
1–2 tsp chopped red chilli
6 tbs very finely-chopped chives, parsley and dill
6 anchovy fillets, cut into tiny cubes
1 small gherkin, sliced into small cubes
oil and vinegar
freshly-ground salt and pepper

Mix the cheese with the crème fraîche and the mustard, then add the herbs, the anchovies and the gherkin. Add the vinegar and oil to taste and let the sauce stand to draw out the flavours for about an hour. Add salt and pepper to taste before serving. Serve with fried fish in breadcrumbs.

Serves 4

GARLIC CREAM

2 peeled cloves garlic
100 ml (3½ fl oz) mayonnaise (see page 12)
100 ml (3½ fl oz) quark
½ tsp powdered saffron
½–1 tsp finely-chopped red chilli
salt and pepper

Crush the garlic and stir into the mayonnaise. Mix in the quark, then add the saffron, the chilli and salt and pepper to taste. Let the cream stand for about an hour to allow the flavours to combine. Serve with poached fish, especially turbot and cod.

Serves 4

RÉMOULADE SAUCE

200 ml (7 fl oz) sour cream, 2 tbs mayonnaise (see page 12), 2–3 tbs chopped pickled cucumber, 1 tbs capers, 2 tbs chopped fresh parsley, 1 tsp dried chervil.

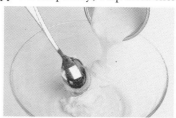

Mix together the sour cream and mayonnaise.

Add the cucumber, capers and parsley.

Mix in the chervil. Serve with fried or grilled fish.

Serves 4

HOLLANDAISE SAUCE

155 g (5½ oz) butter, 3 egg yolks, 2 tbs water or dry white wine, ¼ tsp white pepper, fresh lemon juice and salt if desired.

Melt the butter slowly in a pan over a low heat, then set aside.

Whisk the egg yolks and the water or wine in another saucepan. Place it into a bain marie i.e. put it into a larger saucepan containing hot water. Do not allow the water to boil. Whisk thoroughly until the mixture begins to thicken.

Next add the melted butter slowly, whisking vigorously all the time. Add the pepper, lemon juice and salt to taste, if needed. Ideal for all types of poached fish.

Serves 4

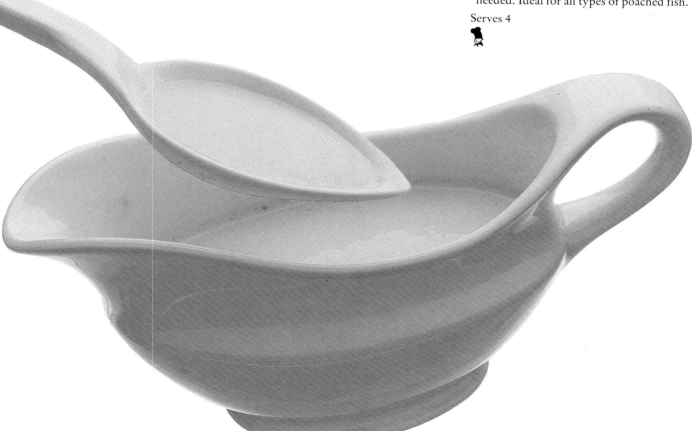

WHITE SAUCE

400 ml (14 fl oz) milk, 100 ml (3½ fl oz) single cream, 3–6 tbs beurre manié (see page 13), white pepper or Tabasco sauce, salt.

Mix the milk and the cream in a saucepan and bring to the boil. Whisk in the beurre manié bit by bit.

Continue to cook, whisking continuously for 3–5 minutes, until shiny.

For an unblemished smooth white sauce, use Tabasco instead of white pepper. Add salt to taste.
Serve with white fish.

Serves 4–6

FOUR FLAVOURED SAUCES

The following are suggestions for flavourings to add to the basic white sauce:

Meaux mustard sauce – stir in 1–2 tbs Meaux (or grain) mustard.

Egg sauce – chop up 2 hard-boiled eggs and mix into the sauce.

Parsley sauce – mix the sauce with 3 tbs finely-chopped fresh parsley.

Horseradish sauce – add 3–4 tbs of grated horseradish to the sauce, then stir in 1 tsp sugar and 1 tsp vinegar.
All these sauces are ideal with steamed or poached fish.

Serves 4

LEMON JUICE

1 well-washed lemon, 70 g (2½ oz) butter at room temperature, water if necessary.

Fry the chosen fish in a large frying pan, remove and keep warm. Grate the peel from half the lemon into the pan.

Squeeze the lemon juice out of the whole lemon and add most of the juice to the pan.

Whisk in the soft butter bit by bit. Dilute with a little water if necessary. Add the rest of the lemon juice to taste. Serve the sauce immediately.

Serves 4

White Sauce

Meaux Mustard Sauce

OLIVE AND TOMATO SAUCE

10–12 olives, 1–2 tbs spicy tomato ketchup, 1 tsp potato flour, 200 ml (7 fl oz) whipping cream.

Slice the olives.

Put the olives, the ketchup and the potato flour into a saucepan. Stir in the cream.

Bring the sauce to the boil, stirring continuously.
This is a delicious sauce for poached fish, particularly plaice or cod.

Serves 4

PINK PEPPERCORN SAUCE

100 ml (3½ fl oz) fish stock, 200 ml (7 fl oz) crème fraîche, 1 tsp crushed pink peppercorns, ½ tsp salt.

Boil the fish stock in a saucepan.

Reduce the heat and add the crème fraîche bit by bit.

Let the sauce cook for 5–10 minutes, uncovered. Stir in the pink peppercorns and the salt and serve with steamed or poached fish, particularly plaice.

Serves 4

SWEET AND SOUR SAUCE

2 tbs butter
2 tbs flour
285 ml (10 fl oz) milk
100 ml (3½ fl oz) fish stock
1 tsp white vinegar
2 tsp sugar
salt and pepper

Melt the butter in a saucepan. Stir in the flour and cook for 1–2 minutes. Mix in the milk, little by little, then let the sauce bubble for 3–5 minutes, as you stir. Add the stock, the white vinegar and the sugar. Season to taste with salt and pepper. Serve with poached fish, particularly cod.

Serves 4

Egg Sauce

Parsley Sauce

Horseradish Sauce

SOLE WITH WHITE WINE SAUCE

4 sole fillets, total weight about 680 g
(1½ lb), skinned
100 ml (3½ fl oz) dry white wine
100 ml (3½ fl oz) fish stock
1 shallot, chopped
a few sprigs parsley
a few knobs of butter
400 ml (14 fl oz) whipping cream
2–3 tbs beurre manié (see page 13)
freshly-squeezed lemon juice
cayenne pepper or Tabasco sauce
a few drops Worcestershire sauce
salt, if needed

Place the sole fillets into a shallow
ovenproof dish with the dry white wine, the
fish stock, the onion and the parsley. Dot
with butter and poach in the oven at 180 °C/
350 °F/Gas Mark 4 for 15–20 minutes.
Meanwhile, cook the cream until thickened
slightly. Watch the cream carefully, so that
it doesn't overcook. When the fish is ready,
transfer to a heated serving platter and keep
warm. Sieve the stock and boil rapidly until
reduced to approximately the same quantity
as the cream. Thicken the stock with the
beurre manié, whisked in little by little.
When the consistency is as thick as the
reduced cream, mix both together. Add the
lemon juice and the cayenne pepper or
Tabasco to taste. Stir in a few drops of
Worcestershire sauce and add a little salt if
necessary. For a glossy finish, stir in a little
cold butter. Pour the sauce over the fish
fillets and serve.
This is very good with rice.

Serves 4

BEURRE BLANC WITH CREAM

3 shallots
2 tbs white wine vinegar
55 ml (2 fl oz) white wine or water
100 ml (3½ fl oz) whipping cream
255 g (9 oz) butter
salt and pepper
freshly-squeezed lemon juice, if necessary

Chop up the shallots very finely. Put the
onion, the vinegar, the wine or water into a
saucepan. Bring to the boil and boil rapidly
until there are only about 2–3 tbs left. Sieve
to remove onion if desired. Add the cream
and the butter bit by bit, whisking
vigorously. Stir in the salt, pepper and
possibly lemon juice to taste.
This is a traditional butter sauce in a
modern manner. By adding a little cream to
the sauce, there is less risk that the sauce
will curdle when you prepare it or keep it
warm.
This is an ideal sauce for steamed or grilled
fish.

Serves 6–8

CHEESE SAUCE

2 tbs butter
2 tbs flour
500 ml (about 18 fl oz) milk
740 g (5 oz) grated, hard cheese
¼ tsp white pepper
salt, if necessary
2 tbs cream or crème fraîche, if desired

Melt the butter in a saucepan. Stir in the
flour and cook for 1–2 minutes. Gradually
stir in a third of the milk and whisk
thoroughly. Stir in the rest of the milk and
cook for about 5 minutes. Mix in the cheese,
with the pepper and a little salt if needed.
Add a little cream or crème fraîche, if
desired. This is delicious with all types of
boiled fish. It is also good as a gratin sauce.

There are 2 variations of this sauce: you can
replace 100 ml (3½ fl oz) milk with the same
quantity of white wine and you can make it
with peppers to add texture. Add finely-
chopped red or green peppers to the sauce.

Serves 4–5

SHRIMP SAUCE

100 g (3½ oz) fresh shrimps
2 shallots
155 g (5½ oz) unsalted butter
55 ml (2 fl oz) white wine vinegar
100 ml (3½ fl oz) white wine
100 ml (3½ fl oz) whipping cream
freshly-ground white pepper

Shell the shrimps and rinse the shells. Chop the onion finely and soften it in a little of the butter. Add the vinegar, wine and the shrimp shells. Bring the mixture to the boil and cook for 3 minutes, then add the cream. Cook for another 3 minutes. Sieve the sauce carefully. Put the shelled shrimps with the rest of the butter into a food processor. Process until smooth. Bring the sauce to the boil again, then remove from the heat and whisk in the shrimp purée. Warm up the sauce but do not let it boil. Add pepper to taste.
This sauce is particularly good with poached fish.

Serves 4–5

SAFFRON SAUCE

½ onion
2 tbs butter
2 tbs flour
500 ml (about 18 fl oz) fish stock
good pinch of powdered saffron
100 ml (3½ fl oz) sour cream
salt and pepper

Finely chop the onion and simmer it gently in the butter. Sprinkle over the flour and cook for 1–2 minutes. Gradually stir in one third of the fish stock and whisk thoroughly. Stir in the rest of the stock and cook for 5 minutes, then add the saffron and the sour cream. Heat the sauce through. Add salt and pepper to taste.
This sauce is excellent with steamed or poached plaice or salmon.

Serves 6

CHIVE SAUCE

100 ml (3½ fl oz) white wine
100 ml (3½ fl oz) fish stock
200 ml (7 fl oz) crème fraîche
½ tsp salt
¼–½ tsp white pepper
6 tbs finely-chopped chives
1 tbs butter

Mix the wine and the fish stock in a saucepan and bring to the boil. Stir in the crème fraîche bit by bit. Cook the sauce for 10–15 minutes over a high heat, whisking now and again. Add salt and pepper to taste. Add the chives and the butter bit by bit. Heat the sauce through and serve with poached fish, particularly plaice, perch or salmon.

Serves 4

BUTTER SAUCE WITH BEER

1 kg (2¼ lb) fish with bones or 680 g (1½ lb) without
155 g (5½ oz) unsalted butter
4 finely-chopped shallots
285 ml (10 fl oz) fish stock
100 ml (3½ fl oz) lager or light ale
salt and freshly-ground pepper
1 tbs finely-chopped chives

Fry the fish gently in a little of the butter together with the onion but do not let the onion brown. Pour in the beer and the fish stock. Let the whole mixture simmer gently for 5–10 minutes. Using a slotted spoon, transfer the fish to a heated serving platter and keep warm. Continue to cook the sauce for a few more minutes, then whisk in the butter. Add salt and pepper to taste. Sprinkle over the finely-chopped chives.

Serves 4

RED PEPPER SAUCE

2 red peppers
butter
1 quantity beurre blanc (see page 13)
salt and freshly-ground pepper
cayenne pepper

Cut the peppers in half, remove the stalks, membranes and seeds and divide each pepper into 8–10 pieces. Fry the pepper carefully in a little butter, then transfer to a food processor and process to a smooth purée. Return to the pan and gradually whisk in the beurre blanc. Add salt and pepper to taste.
Pour this sauce over poached fish.

Serves 4

ROE SAUCE

fish bones
4 white peppercorns
parsley sprigs
water
100 ml (3½ fl oz) dry white wine
200 ml (7 fl oz) crème fraîche
white pepper
cayenne pepper
3–4 tbs red lumpfish roe
salt

Put the fish bones, white peppercorns and parsley into a saucepan. Pour over enough water to cover. Bring to the boil and cook for 20 minutes, then sieve the stock and boil rapidly until reduced to about 100 ml (3½ fl oz). Mix the stock with the wine and the crème fraîche. Reduce the sauce over a high heat, for 5–10 minutes. Season with white pepper and cayenne pepper, then stir in the lumpfish roe. Add salt if necessary.
Serve this delightful sauce with plaice or lemon sole.

Serves 4

TURBOT

Sole, halibut, brill, plaice, flounder and dab
are all tasty varieties of flat fish but perhaps
the most delicious is turbot, which is
available all year round from specialist
fishmongers. Check that the fish's eyes are
protruding slightly and that the gills are a
dark red: this is a sign that the fish is fresh.
The flesh should be hard and there should
be a little mucus on the outside. It should
have a mild and pleasant smell. Turbot are
sold whole or in steaks or fillets. Chicken
turbot are a small version of this grand fish,
weighing 1–1¼ kg (2–3 lb). Try the fish
baked in foil and serve with a suitable sauce.

ABOUT HERBS AND SPICES

Herbs and spices used singly or in combination are indispensable for a good sauce, whether as flavour enhancers or, used in larger quantities, as the focal point. However, they should be used in moderation, particularly if you are using them for the first time. Too many herbs or spices will overpower the flavour and the damage is difficult to repair (see page 100). Experiment with unfamiliar flavourings, using them sparingly at first, then gradually increasing the amount until you achieve the flavour which suits you. The appeal of herbs and spices is very personal, so it is not possible to single out any one as being the best: all come into their own in certain circumstances. However, there are certain herbs and spices which are commonly used in sauces and these are described here, beginning with pepper, probably the most popular of all flavourings.

There are basically four different types of peppercorns: black, white, green and pink. The first three are all fruits of the same tropical vine. White pepper is made from shelled, mature peppercorns. It is not as strong as black pepper, which has both the shell and the kernel from the unripe fruit. Green peppercorns are the fresh fruit of this vine. White pepper and black pepper are particularly useful in sauces, so have them always to hand. They have a more marked taste if freshly ground. Lemon pepper is normal black pepper with a lemon aroma. Pink peppercorns are the fruits of an entirely different tree, native to South America. They have a lively and delicious taste, particularly suited to fish sauces but should be used with caution as some people suffer a highly allergic reaction to them.

Allspice belongs to a different family which is related to cloves. It gives a fine flavour to sauces and pickles.

Red chilli pepper, cayenne pepper and paprika all belong to the capsicum family. The first two are very strong, so use them cautiously.

Curry powder is a mixture of many hot and aromatic spices, such as pepper, ginger, coriander, nutmeg, cardamon, turmeric (which gives the characteristic yellow colour) and cumin. There are many different commercial varieties available from mild to very hot.

Garlic is perhaps the most fantastic of the herbs. It can vary immensely in taste and strength, depending on where the bulb has come from, how long it has been cooked for and how it is prepared. Crush the garlic if you like a strong taste or, if you prefer a weaker taste, chop it very finely. Garlic is easy to grow and is found wild in many parts of the country. Try planting a few cloves and very soon you will see narrow green leaves pushing their way up: these taste very mildly of garlic.

Basil you can also grow yourself, either in the garden or in a pot on the windowsill. Thyme, rosemary and sage are also easy to grow. Buy them as seedlings from a nursery or try growing them from seeds.

Dill, chives and parsley are particularly delicious and useful. Choose the flat-leaved continental parsley for a stronger flavour. The more finely you chop these three herbs, the finer the taste. A food processor is ideal for obtaining this fineness.

Tarragon is one of the few herbs which are better dried than fresh. Its distinctive yet subtle flavour can be used to advantage in a wide range of sauces to complement almost all types of food.

Finally, if using dried herbs, remember to keep them in airtight containers, away from light and heat sources, to preserve their fine flavour and their fresh smell. The same applies to spices. Buy small containers and do not keep them for too long, as they deteriorate with time.

SAUCES FOR SEAFOOD

DILL AND CHIVE SAUCE

200 ml (7 fl oz) sour cream or crème fraîche
1 tbs grated horseradish
1 tbs mustard
2 tbs finely-chopped chives
2 tbs finely-chopped fresh dill
salt and freshly-ground white pepper
freshly-squeezed lemon juice, if desired

Mix the ingredients together. Add salt,
pepper or lemon juice to taste.
Serve with lobster or crayfish.

Serves 4

SAFFRON AND PAPRIKA SAUCE

200 ml (7 fl oz) sour cream
2 tbs mayonnaise
1 tsp paprika powder
¼ tsp powdered saffron
¼ tsp black pepper
½ tsp salt
½ tsp sugar
1 tsp cognac, if desired

Whisk together the sour cream and the
mayonnaise. Stir in the paprika, saffron and
pepper. Add salt, sugar and cognac to taste.
Chill the sauce for a few hours before
serving.
Serve as a dip for prawns.

Serves 4

LOW FAT SHELLFISH SAUCE

255 g (9 oz) quark, 1 tbs vinegar, 1 tbs
sugar, 1½ tbs mustard, 3 tbs finely-chopped
fresh dill, pepper and skimmed milk.

Mix the quark, vinegar, sugar and mustard
together in a bowl.

Stir in the dill.

Add pepper to taste and if the sauce is too
thick, dilute it a little with skimmed milk.
This is delicious with all sorts of shellfish
and also with salmon.

Serves 4–6

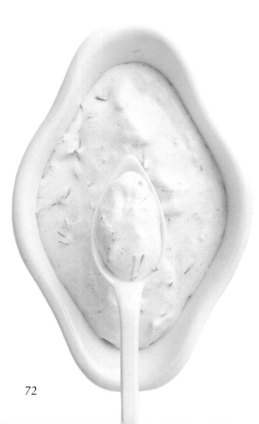

SPICY TOMATO SAUCE

200 ml (7 fl oz) sour cream, 2 tbs mayonnaise, 2 tbs tomato purée, 1 peeled clove garlic, ¼ tsp black pepper, Tabasco sauce.

Mix together the sour cream, the mayonnaise and the tomato purée.

Squeeze the garlic through a press into the mixture.

Season with the pepper and the Tabasco. Chill the sauce for 20 minutes before serving.
Serve with prawns or crab.

Serves 4

DIABOLO

2 tbs crushed green peppercorns, 1 tbs brown sauce, 1 tsp mustard (mild and sugar free), 1 tsp vinegar, 6 drops Tabasco sauce, 200 ml (7 fl oz) sour cream.

Mix together the peppercorns, brown sauce, mustard, vinegar and Tabasco.

Add the sour cream.

Mix well and the sauce is ready to serve. The sauce can be mixed directly in the serving bowl if necessary.
Serve with shellfish.

Serves 4

RHODE ISLAND SAUCE

200 ml (7 fl oz) sour cream or crème fraîche, 1 tsp chilli sauce, 1 tsp mustard (preferably mild and sugar free), ½ tsp paprika powder, 3 drops Tabasco sauce, 1–2 tbs whisky.

Put the crème fraîche or the sour cream into a food processor.

Add the chilli sauce, mustard, paprika powder, Tabasco and whisky.

Process until the sauce becomes completely smooth.
Serve with all types of shellfish.

Serves 4

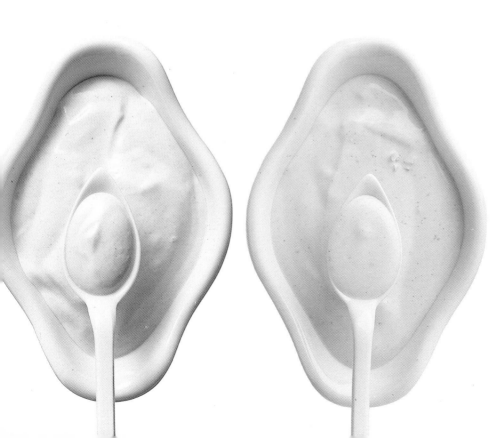

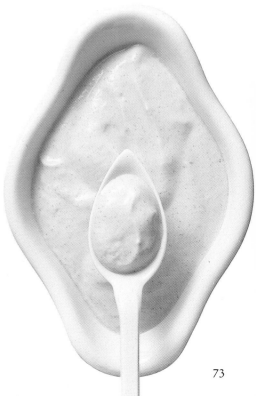

GARLIC SAUCE FOR PRAWNS

2 tsp potato flour, ¼ tsp white pepper, 1 tbs mustard, 285 ml (10 fl oz) whipping cream, 1–2 cloves garlic, 6 tbs finely-chopped fresh dill, 1 kg (2¼ lb) prawns with their shells (300–400 g/11–14 oz shelled), salt, if desired.

Mix the flour, the pepper, the mustard and the cream together in a saucepan. Squeeze in the garlic. Stir thoroughly.

Bring to the boil, whisking all the time. Remove from the heat and mix in the dill.

Finally, mix in the prawns. Warm the sauce but do not let it boil. Serve on toast.

Serves 4

MEXICAN PRAWN SAUCE

1 × 210 g (7½ oz) can sliced mushrooms, 2 chopped onions, 1–2 tbs butter, 1 tbs flour, 1 sliced green pepper, 100 ml (3½ fl oz) tomato ketchup, 1 tsp salt, ¼ tsp white pepper, ¼ tsp cayenne pepper, 3 tbs concentrated frozen orange juice, thawed, 100 ml (3½ fl oz) water, 200 ml (7 fl oz) single cream, 1 kg (2¼ lb) shelled prawns.

Drain the liquid from the mushrooms. Simmer the onions and the mushrooms in the butter. Sprinkle over the flour and stir.

Stir in the green pepper, the ketchup, salt, white and cayenne pepper, orange juice, water and the cream. Cook for 10 minutes.

Add the shelled prawns.
Serve this sauce with boiled rice.

Serves 4

BASIL BUTTER SAUCE

1 quantity beurre blanc (see page 11)
6 leaves fresh basil
freshly-ground pepper, if desired.

Put the beurre blanc into a food processor or a liquidizer with the basil. Process until it is smooth. Add a little extra pepper if desired. If fresh basil is unobtainable, substitute another fresh herb rather than using dried basil.
Serve with crayfish or scampi.

Serves 4

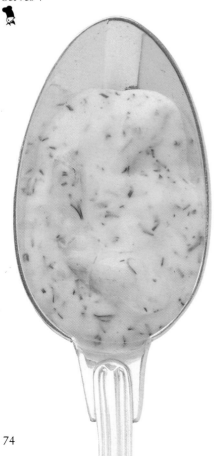

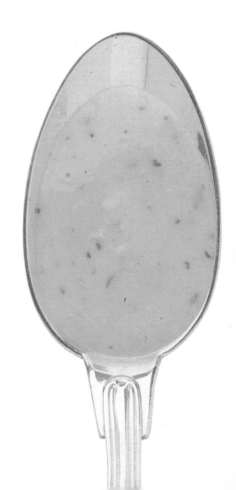

COULIS ORIENTAL

1 leek
2 tbs butter
4 tomatoes
2 red peppers
1 tsp curry powder
1 tbs short grain rice
285 ml (10 fl oz) milk
200 ml (7 fl oz) water
salt and pepper

Slice the leek very finely. Fry it slowly in the butter without browning. Dip the tomatoes into boiling water for 10 seconds, then skin them and chop roughly. Chop the pepper into cubes of about 1 cm (½ in). Put all the ingredients into a saucepan, bring to the boil and cook for about 25 minutes. Cool slightly, transfer to a food processor or liquidizer and process until smooth. Add salt and pepper to taste.
Serve with mussels.

Serves 4

WALNUT SAUCE

200 ml (7 fl oz) crème fraîche or sour cream
1 tbs finely-chopped gherkins
1 tbs chopped walnuts
salt and freshly-ground white pepper
a little juice from the gherkins, if desired

Mix the crème fraîche or the sour cream with the gherkins and the walnuts. Add salt, pepper, and a little of the gherkin liquid to taste.
Good with lobster.

Serves 4

ITALIAN SHELLFISH SAUCE

5 tomatoes
3 shallots
3 tbs butter
½ tsp thyme
100 ml (3½ fl oz) white wine
100 ml (3½ fl oz) whipping cream
pepper

Dip the tomatoes into boiling water for about 10 seconds, then skin them and chop roughly. Finely chop the shallots and simmer them in butter with the thyme until softened. Add the wine, increase the heat and boil until almost evaporated. Add the cream and the chopped tomatoes and heat through. Pepper well and serve with hot mussels or other hot shellfish dishes.

Serves 4

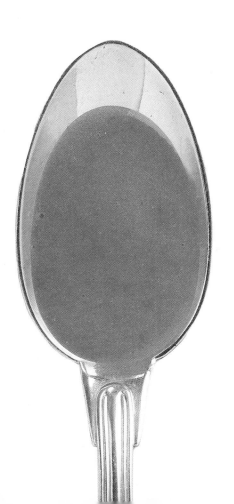

GOURMET SAUCE WITH FLAMBÉED SHELLFISH

1–2 shallots
310 g (11 oz) fresh mushrooms
butter
1 peeled clove garlic, if desired
approx. 300 g (11 oz) boiled crayfish tails
or 1 kg (2¼ lb) prawns in their shells
2 tbs cognac
2 tbs Pernod
200 ml (7 fl oz) whipping cream, lightly whipped
1 × 310 ml (11 fl oz) can lobster soup
3 tbs finely-chopped fresh parsley
2–3 tsp dried tarragon
5–8 tbs Hollandaise Sauce (approx. ½ quantity, see page 63)

Finely chop the onions and slice the mushrooms. Simmer the onion and the mushrooms in a little butter over a low heat in a shallow pan. Squeeze in the garlic through a press, if using. Add the shellfish and heat the whole mixture gently. Pour in the spirits and ignite carefully. When the flame has died out, stir in the cream and the lobster soup. Cook for a few minutes, then add the parsley and crumble in the tarragon. Take the pan off the heat and stir in the Hollandaise sauce. Serve with rice.

Serves 6

CRAB FRICASSÉ WITH DILL SAUCE

400 ml (14 fl oz) whipping cream
4 small boiled crabs
2 tomatoes
1 leek
1 bunch fresh dill
salt and white pepper

Boil the cream until it is reduced by half. Remove from the heat. Take out the white and brown crab meat and reserve. Discard the stomach sac and grey-feathered gills. Scrub the shells thoroughly. Scald the tomatoes and skin them. Slice the tomatoes and leek into cubes and finely chop the dill. Stir the crab meat into the warm cream and heat the mixture through. Mix in the vegetables, then add salt and pepper to taste. Put this filling into the crab shells. Serve with toast.

Serves 4

HOT OYSTERS WITH LEEKS

12 oysters
100 ml (3½ fl oz) dry white wine
155 ml (5½ fl oz) single cream
55 g (2 oz) butter
green part of a leek
freshly-ground salt and white pepper

Open the oysters and take out the flesh carefully. Keep all the oyster juice and pour it into a saucepan. Add the wine. Add the oysters and heat gently. Using a slotted spoon, take the oysters out and set aside. Strain the stock into a clean saucepan, add the cream and bring to the boil. Lower the heat. Whisk in the butter, slice the leek into small pieces and fold into the sauce with the oysters. Add salt and pepper to taste. These oysters are excellent as an appetizer. Serve them hot in their shells.

Serves 4

LOBSTERS

To ensure maximum freshness and flavour, lobsters should be bought live. They should be active and should bend their tails in under their bodies when you lift them up. The males have more flesh and are a little larger than the females, but the females sometimes have roe, which is excellent boiled. The roe turns red when it is cooked, as does the rest of the lobster. Lobsters make delicious salads, soups and sauces or can be eaten boiled or in a gratin with a herb sauce.

SAUCES FOR PASTA

FENNEL SAUCE

approx. 340 g (12 oz) fennel
1 peeled chopped clove garlic
2 tbs chopped onion
2–3 tbs chopped frozen spinach, thawed
bunch of fresh parsley
100 ml (3½ fl oz) whipping cream
100 ml (3½ fl oz) crème fraîche
3 tbs grated Parmesan or 100 g (3½ oz)
grated hard cheese
freshly-ground salt and pepper

Prepare the fennel and cut it into pieces. Put them into a saucepan, add water and cook for about 25 minutes. Drain off the water and reserve. Simmer the garlic and the onion in a little butter until softened. Add the fennel and the spinach and heat through. Place the parsley in a food processor or liquidizer and process until fine, then add the fennel, onion and spinach. Dilute with about 6 tbs of the reserved cooking liquid. Process again until completely smooth. Return to the saucepan, heat through, then add the cream. Let the mixture cook for another few minutes, then add the crème fraîche and the cheese. Add salt and pepper to taste.
Serve this fennel sauce with tagliatelle and mussels.

Serves 4–6

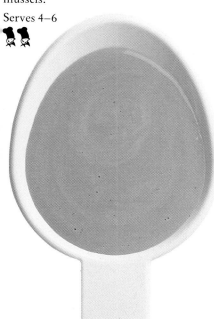

SALMON SAUCE WITH AVOCADO

3–4 shallots
butter
100 g (3½ oz) smoked salmon, chopped
400 ml (14 fl oz) whipping cream
2 tbs unsalted butter
salt and freshly-ground white pepper
2 avocados
100 g (3½ oz) smoked salmon in slices (12 small thin slices)
freshly-cooked pasta bows
3 tbs Parmesan or 100 g (3½ oz) grated hard cheese
truffles, if desired

Chop the onions and simmer in a little butter. Add the chopped salmon and the cream. Bring to the boil and cook for about 10 minutes, stirring constantly. Stir in the butter and salt and pepper to taste. Slice the avocados into 12 pieces. Allow 3 slices of salmon per person. Wrap the salmon pieces round the avocado and warm them in the oven at 150 °C/300 °F/Gas Mark 2 for 4–5 minutes. Place the freshly-cooked pasta on individual serving plates and sprinkle over the cheese. Place the salmon rolls on the plates and pour over the sauce. Garnish with truffles if desired.

Serves 4

TOMATO SAUCE

. 8 tomatoes
1 onion
butter
1 tbs white wine vinegar
freshly-ground salt and pepper
310 g (11 oz) butter at room temperature

Scald and skin the tomatoes. Chop them roughly. Chop the onion finely and simmer in a little butter until softened. Add the tomatoes and cook together over a medium heat for 2–3 minutes. Add the vinegar and salt and pepper to taste. Add the butter bit by bit, whilst whisking vigorously. The sauce should not boil or it may well curdle. Serve with plain or spinach tagliatelle.

Serves 8–10

VEGETABLE SAUCE

2 carrots (approx. 155 g/5½ oz), 125 g (4½ oz) broccoli, thawed if frozen, 3 tbs fresh parsley, 285 ml (10 fl oz) vegetable stock, 200 ml (7 fl oz) whipping cream, ½ tsp salt and ¼ tsp white pepper.

Peel and slice the carrots. Cook them in boiling salted water for 10 minutes.

Add the broccoli and let these vegetables cook for a further 5–8 minutes.

Chop the parsley finely in a food processor.

Drain the vegetables, reserving some of the water, and transfer to the food processor. Dilute with a little of the water and the cream and process until finely-chopped. Add salt and pepper and serve with freshly-cooked pasta.

Serves 4–6

PICNIC SAUCE

200 ml (7 fl oz) sour cream, 6–8 anchovy fillets, 1 peeled clove garlic, 1 tbs tomato ketchup, ½ tsp dried rosemary, pepper and 1 tbs capers.

Place all the ingredients except for the capers in a liquidizer.

Run the liquidizer until the mixture becomes smooth and add pepper to taste.

Stir in the capers.
This is good with cold pasta.

Serves 4

GREEN PEA PURÉE

1 × 225 g (8 oz) frozen green peas, thawed, 100 ml (3½ fl oz) vegetable stock, 200 ml (7 fl oz) whipping cream, 1–2 tsp lemon juice, ½ tsp salt, ¼ tsp white pepper, 1 × 340 g (12 oz) jar mussels.

Process the peas with the stock in a food processor, then add the cream.

Add the lemon, salt and pepper.

Cook the chosen pasta. Drain the mussels and pour the sauce and the mussels over the pasta. Stir and heat through. Serve with grated cheese.

Serves 4

DILL SAUCE WITH PRAWNS

2 apples, 1 onion, 1 peeled clove garlic, butter, 1–2 tsp tomato purée, 100 ml (3½ fl oz) white wine or vegetable stock, 200 ml (7 fl oz) whipping cream, 6 tbs chopped fresh dill, salt and pepper, 25–30 peeled prawns.

Slice the apples into cubes and finely chop the onion.

Simmer the apples, the onion and the garlic in a little butter until softened.

Mix in the tomato purée and dilute with the wine or stock and the cream.

Heat the sauce gently, then lower the heat and stir in the dill. Add salt and pepper to taste. Add the prawns and stir. Pour the sauce over freshly-cooked pasta.

Serves 4

QUARK SAUCE

225 g (8 oz) quark, 55 ml (2 fl oz) crème fraîche, if desired, 1 tbs grated hard cheese, particularly Parmesan, 1 tsp dried oregano, ½ tsp grated nutmeg, milk, if desired.

Mix together the quark and the crème fraîche.

Add the cheese, the oregano and the nutmeg. Stir thoroughly.

Dilute with milk, if a thinner sauce is preferred.
Serve with cold pasta as a salad.

Serves 4–6

HAM SAUCE

100 g (3½ oz) Bayonne ham, 200 ml (7 fl oz) sour cream, 1 tbs finely-chopped chives, 1 tsp mild mustard, ½ tsp Italian salad seasoning.

Slice the Bayonne ham into small cubes and mix with the sour cream.

Cut the chives directly into the mixture.

Flavour with the mustard and the salad seasoning.
Serve with cold pasta as a salad.

Serves 4

TOMATO SAUCE WITH GARLIC

6 tomatoes, 2 shallots, 2 peeled cloves garlic, 55 g (2 oz) butter, 1 tsp dried oregano, 100 ml (3½ fl oz) whipping cream, salt and pepper.

Scald the tomatoes in boiling water and skin.

Remove the seeds and chop roughly. Finely chop the shallots and the garlic.

Simmer the garlic and the shallots in the butter until softened.

Add the oregano, the tomatoes and the cream. Cook the sauce until heated through, then add salt and pepper to taste. Serve with hot pasta.

Serves 3

BLUE CHEESE SAUCE

100–125 g (3½–4½ oz) blue cheese, 200 ml (7 fl oz) crème fraîche, ¼ tsp black pepper, 3 tbs finely-chopped parsley.

Cook the chosen pasta until tender. Drain and return to the saucepan. Crumble the blue cheese over the pasta.

Add the crème fraîche and the pepper.

Stir and warm up carefully. Sprinkle with parsley and serve in deep dishes with the pasta.

Serves 4

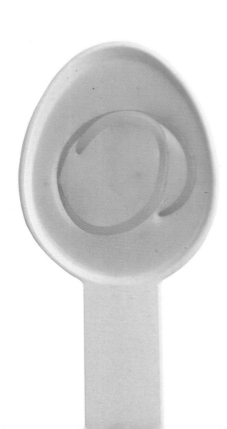

MINCED MEAT SAUCE EXTRA

340 g (12 oz) minced meat, butter, 1 leek, 100 g (3½ oz) smoked ham, salt, pepper, 4 tbs spicy tomato ketchup, 1 tbs soy sauce, 285 ml (10 fl oz) milk, 2 cloves garlic.

Brown the meat in a little butter in a large flameproof casserole or frying pan.

Finely slice the leek and let it brown with the meat. Slice the ham into small cubes.

Add the ham, salt and pepper to taste, ketchup, soy sauce and milk to the meat. Crush the garlic and stir in. Cook for 10–15 minutes, stirring occasionally, until the meat is tender.
Serve with freshly-cooked pasta.

Serves 4

CELERY SAUCE

155 g (5½ oz) celery, butter, 1 peeled clove garlic, 1 tbs roughly-chopped fresh basil, 200 ml (7 fl oz) vegetable stock, 200 ml (7 fl oz) single cream, salt and pepper.

Slice the celery and simmer it in a little butter until soft. Squeeze in the garlic through a press.

Sprinkle the basil over the top.

Dilute with the stock and the cream and bring to the boil. Add salt and pepper to taste.
This is good with freshly-cooked pasta.

Serves 4

LIGURIAN PASTA SAUCE

170 g (6 oz) butter
100 ml (3½ fl oz) quark
3 peeled cloves garlic
1 bunch of fresh parsley
10 leaves of fresh basil
1 tbs grated Parmesan or 55 g (2 oz) grated hard cheese
salt and pepper

Melt the butter gently in a saucepan. Meanwhile, put the rest of the ingredients in a food processor and process to a smooth green sauce. Add this mixture to the melted butter little by little over a gentle heat, whisking all the time. The sauce should not boil. Add salt and pepper to taste. Fold freshly-cooked pasta into the sauce and serve immediately.

Serves 4

PINK CRAYFISH SAUCE

2 tbs finely-chopped onion
butter
3 chopped heads of dill or 1½ tbs dill seeds
2 tbs tomato purée
100 ml (3½ fl oz) fish stock
200 ml (7 fl oz) crème fraîche
salt and white pepper
a little freshly-squeezed lemon juice
12–15 finely-chopped, boiled crayfish tails

Simmer the onion in the butter until soft but not coloured. Add the dill, the tomato purée and the fish stock. Bring the whole mixture to a vigorous boil and let it boil for 3–4 minutes. Lower the heat. Add the crème fraîche and cook for a further 5 minutes. Add salt, pepper and lemon juice to taste. Sieve the sauce, then add the chopped crayfish tails.
Serve immediately with freshly-cooked penne.

Serves 4

MEAT AND CHEESE SAUCE

1 small leek, 200 g (7 oz) pork, butter, 1 peeled clove garlic, 100 ml (3½ fl oz) dry white wine or vegetable stock, 200 ml (7 fl oz) whipping cream, 100 g (3½ oz) grated hard cheese, salt and pepper.

Slice the leek and the meat into thin strips.

Simmer the white parts of the leek and the meat in a little butter. Squeeze in the garlic through a press.

Dilute with the wine or stock and the cream. Cook for 10–15 minutes. Stir in the cheese, then add salt and pepper to taste. Serve with freshly-cooked pasta and garnish with the green pieces from the leek.

Serves 2–3

BACON AND PEPPER SAUCE

1 onion, 155 g (5½ oz) streaky bacon, 2–3 small peppers of different colours, a little turmeric, 200 ml (7 fl oz) stock, preferably chicken stock, 200 ml (7 fl oz) crème fraîche, salt and pepper.

Finely chop the onion. Cut the bacon and the peppers into strips.

Simmer the onion and the bacon in a frying pan and sprinkle over a little turmeric.

Stir in the stock and the crème fraîche.

Stir in the peppers and cook for a few minutes. Add salt and pepper to taste. Wonderful with all types of freshly-cooked pasta.

Serves 4

SALSA PIZZAIOLA

8 ripe tomatoes
4 shallots
6 cloves garlic
4 rolled anchovy fillets
3 green olives stuffed with pimento
70 g (2½ oz) butter
1 tbs capers
1 tsp rosemary
coarsely-grated hard cheese

Scald, skin and take the seeds out of the tomatoes. Chop them, then peel and finely chop the shallots and the garlic. Chop up the anchovies and slice the olives. Cook the onion in the butter, until it becomes light brown, then add the tomato, the shallots, the anchovies, the olives, the capers and the rosemary. Cook the sauce slowly for about 10 minutes. Sprinkle over the grated cheese and serve with penne.

Serves 4

SALMON SAUCE

1 finely-chopped shallot, butter, 200–285 ml (7–10 fl oz) whipping cream, 55 ml (2 fl oz) white wine, 110 g (4 oz) smoked salmon, coarsely-ground black pepper, grated hard cheese.

Simmer shallot in a little butter over a low heat until soft but not browned.

Add the cream and the wine. Cook for 1 minute.

Chop the salmon into small cubes. Heat them up for 10 seconds in a non-stick pan without fat.

Stir the salmon into the sauce and add black pepper to taste. Serve immediately with freshly-cooked pasta. Sprinkle with grated cheese.

Serves 4

ORANGE CHICKEN

1 roasted chicken, 1 red pepper, 1 tbs soy sauce, 3 tbs concentrated frozen orange juice, thawed, 200 ml (7 fl oz) whipping cream, 100 ml (3½ fl oz) chicken stock, curry powder, if desired, salt and pepper.

Bone the chicken and slice the meat into small pieces. Finely chop the pepper.

Mix together the chicken, the red pepper, the soy sauce, the orange juice, the cream and the stock in a saucepan.

Cook for 2–3 minutes until heated through. Add a little curry powder if desired and salt and pepper to taste.
Serve with freshly-cooked pasta.

Serves 4

OLIVE SAUCE

100 g (3½ oz) green olives stuffed with pimento, 100 g (3½ oz) black olives with stones, 2 cloves garlic, peeled and finely-chopped, 100 g (3½ oz) butter, 100–200 ml (3½–7 fl oz) tomato juice.

Chop up the olives roughly. Remove the stones from the black olives.

Simmer the garlic slowly in the butter in a heavy-bottomed saucepan. When both the butter and the garlic begin to brown slightly, pour in the tomato juice.

Bring to the boil, then add the chopped olives. Mix the sauce with freshly-cooked pasta and serve immediately.

Serves 3–4

SALSA POMODORO

8 ripe tomatoes
4 shallots
55 g (2 oz) butter
½ tsp dried marjoram
salt and pepper
200 ml (7 fl oz) crème fraîche

Scald, skin and take the cores out of the tomatoes. Peel and chop the shallots finely. Simmer the shallots slowly in the butter without letting them brown. Add the tomatoes and the marjoram. Boil the sauce and reduce it until it becomes quite thick. Add salt and pepper to taste and, as you serve, place a spoonful of crème fraîche on top of the sauce. Alternatively, the crème fraîche can be mixed into the sauce. Serve with freshly-cooked pasta.

Serves 4

COLD TUNA SAUCE

1 × 210 g (7½ oz) can tuna in brine
200 ml (7fl oz) crème fraîche or sour cream
1 peeled clove garlic
1 egg yolk
1 tbs capers
black pepper

Pour the liquid off the tuna and reserve. Put all the ingredients into a food processor and process to a smooth, thick sauce. If the sauce is too stiff, dilute with the reserved liquid. Add black pepper to taste. Wonderful with cold pasta as a salad.

Serves 4

PARSNIP SAUCE WITH PEAS

2 parsnips, approx. 255 g (9 oz)
200 ml (7 fl oz) vegetable stock
200 ml (7 fl oz) whipping cream
1 tsp salt
¼ tsp black pepper
1 tsp dried marjoram
1 × 110 g (4 oz) pkt frozen green peas, thawed

Peel and chop the parsnips. Cook them in the stock in a covered saucepan until tender (about 10 minutes). Transfer the parsnips and the stock to a food processor and process to a purée. Mix the parsnip purée, cream, salt, pepper, marjoram and green peas together in a saucepan. Cook the sauce for a few minutes. Serve with freshly-cooked pasta.

Serves 4

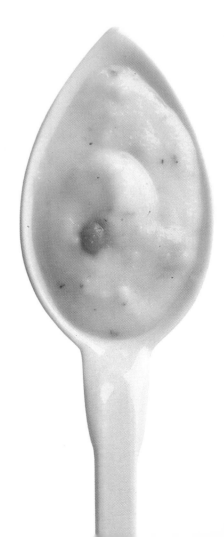

CARROT SAUCE WITH NUTS

3–4 carrots, about 255 g (9 oz)
200 ml (7 fl oz) vegetable stock
200 ml (7 fl oz) crème fraîche or whipping
cream
1 tsp salt
¼ tsp white pepper
½ tsp thyme
6 tbs grated hard cheese
6 tbs chopped hazelnuts or walnuts
milk, if desired

Peel and slice the carrots. Cook them in the
vegetable stock in a covered saucepan for
about 10 minutes, until soft. Transfer the
carrots and the stock to a food processor
and process to a purée. Mix the carrot purée
in a saucepan with the crème fraîche or
cream, the salt, pepper, thyme and cheese.
Cook for a few minutes. Stir in the nuts.
Dilute with a little milk if you prefer a
thinner sauce and serve with freshly-cooked
pasta.

Serves 4

HAM SAUCE WITH OLIVES

200 g (7 oz) smoked ham
10–15 green olives
200 ml (7 fl oz) crème fraîche
2 tsp potato flour
200 ml (7 fl oz) meat or vegetable stock

Cut the ham into small pieces and the olives
into slices. Whisk together the crème fraîche
and the potato flour in a saucepan over a
medium heat. Pour in the stock. Stir in the
ham and the olives and bring the sauce to
the boil.
Serve with freshly-cooked pasta.

Serves 4

MUSHROOM SAUCE WITH GARLIC

400 g (14 oz) mushrooms
butter
1 peeled clove garlic
55 ml (2 fl oz) white wine
200 ml (7 fl oz) single cream
½ tsp salt
¼ tsp black pepper
soy sauce, if desired
6 tbs finely-chopped fresh parsley

Slice the mushrooms and simmer them in a
little butter. Squeeze in the garlic through a
press. Pour in the wine and cream and stir.
Let the sauce boil, uncovered, for about 10
minutes, or until it thickens. Add the salt,
pepper and perhaps the soy sauce to taste.
Stir in the parsley and pour the sauce over
freshly-cooked tagliatelle.

Serves 4

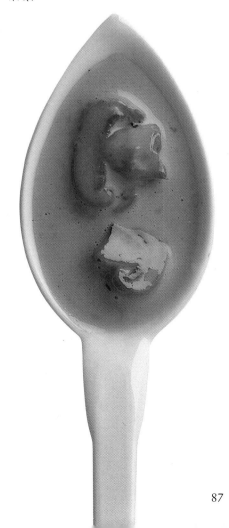

SNAILS IN HERB SAUCE

200 ml (7 fl oz) dry white wine
100 ml (3½ fl oz) fish stock
200 ml (7 fl oz) single cream
6 tbs mixed fresh herbs, e.g. marjoram,
chervil, chives, parsley and basil
55 g (2 oz) butter
2 dozen snails
1 finely-chopped clove garlic
salt and freshly-ground pepper

Bring the wine, fish stock and cream to the
boil. Finely chop the herbs and stir in or
process herbs and liquid in a food
processor. Return to the pan. Whisk in the
butter. Simmer the snails and the garlic in a
little extra butter without letting the garlic
brown. Add to sauce with salt and pepper
to taste. Serve on a bed of freshly-cooked
tagliatelle.

Serves 4

CHANTERELLE SAUCE

500 ml (about 18 fl oz) chicken stock
340 g (12 oz) chanterelles
3 finely-chopped shallots
70 g (2½ oz) butter
salt and freshly-ground pepper

Boil and reduce the stock to half its
quantity. Dry-fry the chanterelles and the
shallots. Whisk the butter into the stock,
then mix in the mushrooms and the onion.
Add salt and pepper to taste. Serve with
fresh pasta (see opposite).

Serves 4

PASTA MARINARA

340 g (12 oz) prawns with shells
a few sprigs parsley
butter
200 ml (7 fl oz) water
2–3 shallots
200 ml (7 fl oz) whipping cream
2 tbs cognac
200 ml (7 fl oz) dry white wine
¼ tsp black pepper
cayenne pepper
beurre manié, if desired (see page 13)
3 tomatoes
approx. 8 boiled crayfish tails
3 tbs finely-chopped fresh parsley

Shell the prawns. Simmer the prawn shells
and the parsley sprigs in a little butter, then
add water. Cook for about 5 minutes. Sieve
the juice, then boil rapidly until reduced to
about 3 tbs. Peel and finely chop the onions
and simmer in a little more butter over a
low heat. Add the prawn juice, cream,
cognac, and the wine. Cook for about 10
minutes. Add the black pepper to taste and
a little cayenne pepper. If the sauce is too
thin, thicken with beurre manié and cook
for a further 3–5 minutes. Scald and skin the
tomatoes. Chop them into small pieces and
mix them into the sauce. Heat the sauce
gently. If necessary, chop the crayfish tails
into pieces. Stir in the prawns, crayfish tails
and parsley. Warm the sauce but do not let
it boil.
Serve immediately with freshly-cooked
pasta.

Serves 4

SAFFRON SAUCE WITH MUSSELS

1 kg (2¼ lb) mussels
3 chopped cloves garlic
6 tbs finely-chopped shallot
butter
100 ml (3½ fl oz) dry white wine
200 ml (7 fl oz) whipping cream
saffron
freshly-ground salt and pepper
100 ml (3½ fl oz) fromage blanc, if desired

Clean and prepare the mussels thoroughly.
Simmer the garlic and the shallot in a
saucepan in a little butter. Add the mussels.
Pour in the wine and stir over a gentle heat.
Cover the saucepan. After about 30 seconds
the mussels will begin to open. This shows
that they are ready. Take the mussels out of
the pan as they open. Discard any that do
not open after a few minutes. Keep the juice
and sieve into another saucepan. Stir in the
cream and boil rapidly until reduced by
half. Lower the heat. Add a little saffron,
salt and pepper to taste, then whisk in the
fromage blanc. Take the mussels out of their
shells and return to the sauce.
Serve with all types of freshly-cooked pasta.

Serves 4

PASTA DOUGH

4 eggs
400 g (14 oz) plain flour
2 tsp oil
½ tsp salt
spinach – for green pasta
tomato purée – for pink pasta

The dough is best blended in a food processor. Process the egg, oil, salt and any flavourings desired for a few seconds. Add the flour while the machine is running, until the dough feels hard and stiff. Rest the dough, then pass through a pasta machine or roll out and cut up by hand.

SAUCES FOR DESSERTS

RASPBERRY PURÉE

100 ml (3½ fl oz) natural yogurt, 225 g (8 oz) fresh raspberries, 1–2 tbs caster sugar.

Put the raspberries and yogurt into a food processor or liquidizer.

Process for a few seconds to a purée. Sieve away the raspberry seeds.

Add a little caster sugar to taste. Serve with fresh berries. The raspberries can also be replaced by blackberries, blackcurrants or strawberries.

Serves 4

STRAWBERRY PURÉE

340 g (12 oz) strawberries, 200 ml (7 fl oz) crème fraîche, 2 tbs caster sugar.

Hull and rinse the strawberries.

Put the strawberries, the crème fraîche and the caster sugar into a food processor.

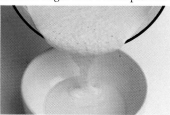

Process to a smooth sauce. Serve with flans or gâteaux.

Serves 4–6

ALMOND QUARK

4 whole almonds in their shells
55 g (2 oz) marzipan
200 ml (7 fl oz) milk
155 ml (5½ fl oz) quark

Scald and shell the almonds. Put the almonds, marzipan and milk in a food processor or a liquidizer and process until the whole mixture is thoroughly mixed. Stir in the quark just before serving.
Ideal with a soft fruit salad.

Serves 4

WHIPPED CREAM

Pour 200–285 ml (7–10 fl oz) double or whipping cream into a round-bottomed bowl.

Whisk with a spiral whisk by hand or with an electric whisk but not for too long, until smooth and fluffy.

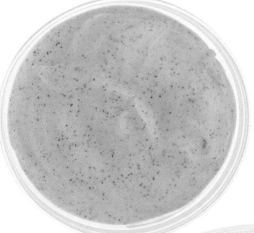

If you have whisked the cream too long, so that it has become porridgy, pour in a little unwhisked cream or milk and gently mix.

Coffee Cream

FOUR WAYS TO FLAVOUR WHIPPED CREAM

Vanilla Sauce: Whisk together 2 egg yolks, 1 tbs caster sugar and 1 tbs vanilla sugar. Fold into the whipped cream.

Rock Cream: Crush 10 small pieces of seaside rock and fold into the whipped cream. Add a little caster sugar if desired.

Orange Cream: Whisk 2 egg yolks with 2 tbs caster sugar and 3 tbs concentrated frozen orange juice, thawed. Fold into the whipped cream.

Coffee Cream: Crush 1 tbs coffee granules and 2–3 tbs caster sugar together in a pestle and mortar. Fold into the whipped cream.

Serves 4–6

COINTREAU CREAM

200 ml (7 fl oz) whipping cream, ¼ lemon, 1–2 tbs Cointreau, 1 tsp caster sugar.

Whip the cream lightly, then put it into the fridge to chill.

Wash the lemon and grate a quarter of the peel.

Squeeze out 1 tsp lemon juice and mix together with the lemon peel, the liqueur and the sugar.

Stir this liqueur mixture quickly into the cream just before serving. This is ideal with fruit, berries and gâteaux or biscuits.

Serves 4–6

Orange Cream

Rock Sauce

GINGER CREAM

200 ml (7 fl oz) whipping cream, 3 pieces of whole crystallized ginger, 3 tbs of the syrup from the ginger, ½ tsp ground ginger.

Whisk the cream lightly, then add the syrup from the ginger.

Slice the ginger itself into very fine strips.

Mix with the cream. Sprinkle a little ground ginger over the cream as you serve it. Delicious with berry fruits and fruit salad.

Serves 4–6

ALMOND CREAM

285 ml (10 fl oz) whipping cream, 2–3 tbs Amaretto (almond liqueur), 2 tbs sugar, 100 g (3½ oz) flaked almonds.

Pour the cream into a bowl. Add the liqueur and the sugar.

Whisk the whole mixture until fluffy.

Dry-roast the flaked almonds carefully in a frying pan.

Fold the almonds carefully into the cream. Serve with fresh or canned peaches.

Serves 6–8

ORANGE SAUCE

2 egg yolks
6 tbs sugar
2 egg whites
2 oranges, peeled
juice and peel of 1 well-washed lemon
200–285 ml (7–10 fl oz) whipping cream

Whisk the egg yolks with the sugar until pale and creamy. Whisk the egg whites in a separate bowl until stiff, then fold them into the egg yolk mixture. Slice the oranges into small pieces and mix them in. Add the lemon juice and the lemon peel. Whip the cream and fold it into the mixture.
Serve the sauce ice-cold with orange desserts.

Serves 6–8

Cointreau Cream

Almond Cream

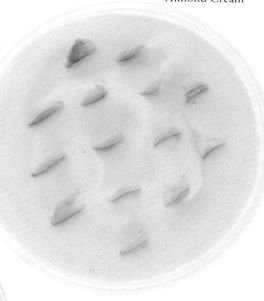

Ginger Cream

SPECIAL CHOCOLATE SAUCE

200 ml (7 fl oz) whipping cream
100 g (3½ oz) dark cooking chocolate
1 tbs vanilla sugar
3 tbs chopped hazelnuts or almonds
3 tbs desiccated coconut

Gently heat up the cream in a saucepan. Break the chocolate into bits and sprinkle them into the cream. Add the vanilla sugar, the nuts and the coconut. Cook the sauce for a few minutes over a low heat, stirring frequently.
This is a wonderful sauce with ice cream and bottled fruit.

Serves 4

QUICK CHOCOLATE SAUCE

200 ml (7 fl oz) whipping cream, 155 g (5½ oz) dark cooking chocolate.

Pour the cream into a saucepan and heat through.

Break the chocolate into pieces and add to the cream.

Reduce the heat and let the chocolate melt slowly. Stir frequently.

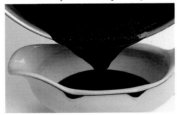

Serve with ice cream, pears or bottled fruit.

Serves 4

CARAMEL CREAM

200 ml (7 fl oz) whipping cream, 2 tbs black treacle or golden syrup, 3 tbs sugar, 1 tbs vanilla sugar, 2 tbs butter.

Pour the cream into a saucepan.

Whisk in the treacle or syrup, the sugar and the vanilla sugar. Bring to the boil.

Whisk in the butter bit by bit and cook over a medium heat until the sauce becomes a little thicker, 5–10 minutes. Serve the sauce warm.
Especially good with ice cream or bottled fruit.

Serves 4

TOFFEE SAUCE

200 ml (7 fl oz) whipping cream, 6 tbs sugar, 6 tbs golden syrup, 100 g (3½ oz) butter, ½ tsp ground ginger, 1 tsp vanilla sugar.

Pour the cream, sugar and syrup into a saucepan. Stir until all is well mixed.

Stir in half the butter.

Let the sauce boil until it has a consistency rather like soft toffee.

Add the ginger, the vanilla sugar and the rest of the butter.
Delicious warm with ice cream.

Serves 4–6

NUT SAUCE

200 ml (7 fl oz) sour cream or quark, 3 tbs hazelnuts or walnuts, 2–4 tbs golden syrup, milk, if desired.

Pour the sour cream or quark into a bowl.

Chop the nuts.

Mix the nuts and the syrup into the cream and, if you want a thinner sauce, dilute with a little milk.
Serve with fruit salad.

Serves 4

SOFT TOFFEE SAUCE

285 ml (10 fl oz) whipping cream, 2 tbs sugar, 1 tsp cocoa powder, ½ vanilla pod or 1 tsp vanilla sugar.

Pour the cream, the sugar and the cocoa powder into a heavy-bottomed saucepan.

Split the vanilla pod lengthways and scrape out the black seeds into the cream.

Cook until the consistency becomes nice and thick. If you use vanilla sugar, mix that in at the last moment.
Serve with ice cream.

Serves 4

WHISKY SAUCE

1 tbs blackcurrant jelly
55 g (2 oz) marzipan
85–100 ml (3–3½ fl oz) whisky
200 ml (7 fl oz) whipping cream

Melt the blackcurrant jelly slowly in a small saucepan. Add the marzipan and take the saucepan off the heat. Mix the marzipan thoroughly with the jelly until completely smooth. Stir in the whisky and leave the sauce to cool. Whisk the cream lightly, then mix the almond mixture with the cream. This is a lovely sauce with pear cooked in red wine.

Serves 4–6

VANILLA CUSTARD SAUCE

4 egg yolks
70 g (2½ oz) sugar
1 vanilla pod
400 ml (14 fl oz) single cream
255 ml (9 fl oz) milk

Whisk the egg yolks with the sugar until pale and creamy. Split the vanilla pod lengthways and scrape out the small seeds. Boil up half the cream and all the milk with the vanilla pod and the seeds. Whisk the eggs with a little of the cream/milk mixture, then pour back into the saucepan. Stir and let the sauce simmer very gently – it must not boil – until it thickens. Leave to cool. Take out the vanilla pod. Whisk the rest of the cream and add when the sauce has cooled.
This sauce is delightful with apple desserts.

Serves 6–8

HOT MINT AND CHOCOLATE SAUCE

3–4 tbs fresh peppermint or mint
200 ml (7 fl oz) water
4–6 tbs cocoa powder
4 tbs sugar
55 g (2 oz) unsalted butter

Chop the mint into very small pieces, including both the stalk and the leaf. Let the mint simmer in the water in a covered pan for 30 minutes. When the water has taken on a strong taste of mint, sieve the liquid off into a clean saucepan. Add the cocoa and the sugar. Bring to the boil and cook for a few minutes until the mixture thickens, then stir in the butter.
This sauce is wonderful with ice cream.

Serves 4

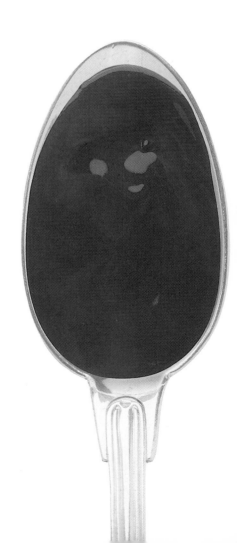

ARRAK SAUCE

200–285 ml (7–10 fl oz) whipping cream
2 egg yolks
1–2 tsp sugar
just under 55 ml (2 fl oz) arrak

Mix all the ingredients together in a stainless steel saucepan and whisk thoroughly. Continue whisking over a gentle heat until the sauce begins to thicken. This sauce is ideal warmed just as it is or you may also serve it cold. Let it cool first before chilling in the fridge.
Delicious with ice cream or raspberries.

Serves 6

DREAM SAUCE

2 tbs butter, 200 ml (7 fl oz) whipping cream, 3 tbs sugar, 1 tbs vanilla sugar.

Melt the butter in a saucepan.

Add the cream and the sugar. Cook for about 10 minutes, stirring now and again.

Finally mix in the vanilla sugar.
Wonderful with berries and fruit, particularly with a mixture of raspberries and peaches.

Serves 4

LEMON QUARK

255 g (9 oz) quark, 4 tbs caster sugar, 1 tbs vanilla sugar, juice of ½–1 lemon.

Mix the quark, the caster sugar and the vanilla sugar together in a bowl.

Squeeze the juice out of the lemon.

Mix the lemon juice into quark and chill the mixture for about an hour.
Serve with fruit salad.

Serves 6

CINNAMON SAUCE

285 ml (10 fl oz) whipping cream
285 ml (10 fl oz) milk
2–3 tbs ground cinnamon
6 egg yolks
6–7 tbs sugar

Mix the cream, the milk and the cinnamon in a saucepan and bring to the boil. Take the saucepan off the heat. Put the egg yolks and the sugar into a stainless steel saucepan and whisk vigorously. Stir in the cream/milk mixture and put the saucepan back on the heat. Warm up the sauce as you whisk it. When the first bubbles appear take the saucepan off the heat (the sauce must not boil). Sieve the sauce, then transfer to a food processor or a liquidizer and process. Serve hot with apple desserts of all types.

Serves 6–8

MADAME'S DESSERT SAUCE

285 ml (10 fl oz) whipping cream
1 vanilla pod
6 tbs raisins
1–2 tbs rum
1–4 tbs sugar
3 tbs flaked almonds
4 peaches

Boil up the cream. Split the vanilla pod lengthways and scrape out the black seeds into the cream. Add the vanilla pod and the raisins. Let the mixture cook for about 10 minutes. Take out the vanilla pod and discard. Stir in the rum and the sugar to taste. Cook over a low heat for 5–10 minutes. Dry-roast the almonds carefully in a frying pan. Scald and skin the peaches. Divide them into halves and remove the stones. Arrange them on individual plates and pour over the sauce. Garnish with flaked almonds.

Serves 4

ZABAGLIONE SAUCE

6 egg yolks
4 tbs caster sugar
4 tbs Marsala
100 ml (3½ fl oz) whipping cream

Whisk up the egg yolks, the sugar and the wine in a stainless steel bowl or a small saucepan. Put that into a larger saucepan with hot but not boiling water. Whisk the whole time whilst warming up the mixture until it becomes thick and frothy. Take the saucepan off the heat. Whip the cream lightly and whisk it into the sauce little by little.
Serve the sauce hot or warm with bottled fruit, e.g. pears and apples or also with fresh fruit, e.g. kiwi or pineapple.

Serves 4–6

VANILLA

For an authentic flavouring to a vanilla
sauce you should use a vanilla pod. This is
the dried fruit of an orchid which grows
in Central America. Split the vanilla pod
carefully and cook it in water or cream, so
that it gives off its aromatic flavour. The
small black seeds scattered around in the
vanilla sauce are a sign that you have used
genuine vanilla. Vanilla sauce is delicious
with apple pie and other apple desserts.

HOW TO RESCUE A SAUCE

IF YOUR SAUCE HAS CURDLED. In general, sauces will curdle if there is too much fat or if there are too many acid ingredients. Sauces containing egg yolks are liable to curdle if cooked over too high a heat. Try adding a little water to the sauce and whisking hard, or thicken the sauce with flour paste thickening (see page 13) or beurre manié (see page 13).

A Hollandaise sauce or Béarnaise sauce can curdle when the heat has been too high, or when the butter has been added too quickly. Save the sauce by adding a little ice-cold water and whisking vigorously.

Mayonnaise curdles easily if the oil has been added too quickly but you can sort this out by putting an egg yolk into a clean bowl, then whisking in the curdled mayonnaise little by little. Whisk vigorously and use an electric whisk if you have one.

Vanilla custard sometimes curdles when the heat has been too high. The sauce should only simmer very gently, not boil. There isn't actually very much you can do for a curdled vanilla sauce but if you let the sauce cool, then mix it with whipped cream it does not show so much and the flavour is not affected.

IF YOUR SAUCE IS TOO SALTY. This, of course, is caused by the addition of an excess of salty ingredients, so if a sauce calls for stock, soy sauce, cheese or herb mixtures, add these cautiously as they often contain more salt than one realises.

To correct the saltiness, add cream or crème fraîche. A good tip is to put a raw, peeled potato into the sauce and cook it for 10 minutes, then discard. The potato will absorb some of the salt into its flesh.

IF YOUR SAUCE TASTES BURNT. There is not much you can do with a burnt sauce but try sieving it into another saucepan, then adding cream or crème fraîche, or add a strong flavouring which might mask the burnt taste, such as pepper, blue cheese or cognac.

IF YOUR SAUCE IS TOO THICK. It may well be that it has boiled for too long or that the sauce contains too much flour. To thin the sauce, stir in water, stock, wine, milk, cream or crème fraîche, choosing your diluting liquid according to the other ingredients in your sauce.

IF YOUR SAUCE IS TOO THIN. A sauce can fail to thicken sufficiently because it contains too little flour in proportion to the liquid. Certain ingredients also make the sauce thin, such as onion, citrus fruit and wine. You can remedy this problem by using beurre manié or a flour paste thickening (see page 13). You can also reduce the sauce to the desired consistency by boiling rapidly, provided this will not then cause curdling (see above). Taste the sauce first as any saltiness or spiciness will be intensified by reducing and this may not be desirable.

Mayonnaise becomes thin if you do not whisk sufficiently when the oil is added. To thicken mayonnaise, carry out the same procedure as if it had curdled (see above).

IF YOUR SAUCE IS LUMPY. There are several possible causes for this. It may be that the flour has not been allowed to swell in the butter or there could be too much flour in proportion to the butter. Alternatively, the flour may not have been mixed thoroughly enough with the liquid. Or it could be that the liquid has been added too quickly and you have not stirred enough. To obtain a smooth sauce, press through a wire sieve, then warm up the sauce as you whisk it.

IF YOUR SAUCE IS TOO STRONG. If you add spices to your sauce without first tasting it, you run the risk of getting too strong a flavour. Always soften the strength with a little cream or crème fraîche.

IF YOUR SAUCE IS TASTELESS. Taste your sauce and let your own creativity dictate which herbs or spices should be added. Perhaps it just needs salt and pepper but experiment also with soy sauce or tomato purée, mustard, stock, garlic, wine, cognac, whisky or herbs. If the sauce is too thin and needs to be reduced, then this will automatically intensify the flavours.

GLOSSARY

BAIN MARIE. This is used for dishes which demand an even heating. It consists of an outer pan containing hot water into which a smaller pan containing the ingredients is fitted. The cooking can be done in the oven or on the stove and the water should only simmer.

BÉARNAISE. An egg and butter sauce with a piquant flavour, which comes from the French province of Béarn.

BÉCHAMEL. Louis XIV's head waiter and a famous gourmet. He is renowned for having created the basic white sauce which now bears his name.

BEURRE MANIÉ. Literally kneaded butter. Equal proportions of soft butter and flour are worked together into a paste for thickening sauce (see page 13).

TO BRAISE. The raw ingredient is browned in fat, then the rest of its cooking is carried out in a covered saucepan or casserole in a little liquid.

TO BROWN. To heat up fat until it becomes light brown or to heat up a raw ingredient in the fat until it is coloured.

CAFÉ DE PARIS SAUCE. A spiced butter with the consistency of a sauce. This sauce comes from an eponymous restaurant in Geneva. The original recipe is secret but it is known that there are about 50 ingredients and that the basis of it is a béarnaise sauce.

CHILLI SAUCE. A spicy hot tomato sauce containing chilli peppers. Use with caution.

COULIS. A term the French used to apply to any sauce. Now it tends to denote a sauce made from a fruit or vegetable purée.

CRÈME FRAÎCHE. Cream that has been specially treated, so that it will keep slightly longer. It is thick and has a pleasantly sharp taste.

DIP. A thick cold sauce in which sliced raw vegetables such as cucumber, carrot, green pepper, cauliflower, celery and tomato, or pitta bread or crisps are dipped.

TO DRY-ROAST. This is to heat up and brown such ingredients as, for example, almonds or bread, without using fat.

TO FLAMBÉ. To smother a dish with lighted cognac or liqueur, so that most of the alcohol is burnt off but the aroma remains.

FRICADELLES. Small cooked meatballs usually made of veal mincemeat.

FROMAGE BLANC. A home-made cheese which can be served au naturel with fresh herbs or used as a thickening. To make your own, process 200 ml (7 fl oz) sour cream, 200 ml (7 fl oz) natural yogurt and approximately 100 g (3½ oz) Bel Paese cheese in a food processor. Pour the cheese mixture into a bowl and let it stand at room temperature for about 12 hours, then chill.

FROMAGE FRAIS. A low-fat soft cheese made from skimmed milk. It is fermented for only a short time, has a light texture and creamy taste.

INDIENNE. Used in connection with meat and poultry dishes. Indienne means that boiled rice and curry are included.

MARINATE. To put meat, fish or shellfish into an acidic, spicy liquid which preserves and flavours it.

MEAT JUICES. The liquid which is formed during the frying or grilling of meat.

MOCCA. Often used to indicate that a dish has been flavoured with coffee.

PIMENTO. A tinned, preserved type of pepper.

TO POACH. To simmer. This expression is mostly used in the preparation of fish and egg dishes.

TO POLISH. To add the finishing touch to a sauce by putting in a little butter and whisking the mixture so that the sauce becomes shiny and smooth.

POTATO FLOUR. This is particularly useful for thickening sauces when a clear finish is required. It is available from delicatessens.

QUARK. A low-fat soft cheese made from pasteurized skimmed milk. It is very versatile as it is stable at boiling temperatures.

TO REDUCE. This means to boil away the liquid in a sauce so that its volume is reduced and the taste is concentrated. This is easiest to do using a shallow, wide-bottomed saucepan and a high heat.

ROUX. A thickener consisting of flour and butter. The flour is stirred into melted butter and cooked for 1–2 minutes, before the liquid ingredients are added.

SALSA. The Italian and Spanish expression for sauce.

TO SCALD. This is to put an ingredient into boiling water for a few seconds, so that it is easier to peel afterwards. Almonds can be boiled up in water until their skin loosens. Tomatoes, peaches, plums and all sorts of other skinned fruits can be dipped into boiling water for 10 seconds until the skin loosens and splits.

TO SIMMER. This means to cook ingredients in butter or liquid over a low heat, so that the temperature is held just below boiling point. See POACH.

SPICY TOMATO KETCHUP. If this is unobtainable, add chilli sauce to plain tomato ketchup. The amount added will vary according to taste.

TABASCO SAUCE. A hot spicy sauce which is used for flavouring. It is made in Louisiana in the USA by grinding red chilli peppers, mixing them with salt and ageing this mixture for 3 years in oak whisky barrels. Vinegar is added before the sauce is strained and bottled.

VANILLA SUGAR. To make vanilla sugar, bury a vanilla pod in a jar of granulated sugar. Cover with an airtight lid. Leave for 6 weeks for the flavours to mingle. The jar can be topped up with more granulated sugar as the flavoured sugar is used.

INDEX